Embracing Eternity

D0715499

By the same author

Spirited

Embracing Eternity

*The amazing truth about life after death
that will change your world*

Tony Stockwell

HODDER
MOBIUS

Copyright © 2006 by Tony Stockwell

First published in Great Britain in 2006 by Hodder & Stoughton
A division of Hodder Headline

This paperback edition published in 2007

The right of Tony Stockwell to be identified as the Author
of the Work has been asserted by him in accordance with
the Copyright, Designs and Patents Act 1988.

A Mobius paperback

2

A CIP catalogue record for this title is available from the British Library

ISBN 978 0 340 89794 2
ISBN 0 340 89794 5

Typeset in Sabon by Hewer Text UK Ltd, Edinburgh
Printed and bound by Mackays of Chatham Ltd, Chatham, Kent

Hodder Headline's policy is to use papers that are natural, renewable
and recyclable products and made from wood grown in sustainable forests.
The logging and manufacturing processes are expected to conform
to the environmental regulations of the country of origin.

Hodder & Stoughton Ltd
A division of Hodder Headline
338 Euston Road
London NW1 3BH

Extract from *A Grief Observed* by C.S. Lewis on pages 80–1
reprinted by kind permission of Faber and Faber. © C.S. Lewis

I would like to dedicate this book to
all the great pioneers of spirit communication
whose demonstrating and teaching brilliance
has paved the way for so many of today's workers!

In particular, a special mention to those whose work
has touched me on a personal level, some of whom I have
had the great pleasure of meeting and others of whom
came into my life through books and the wonderful stories
that get passed along the generations.

Joan Barham
Marcia Ford
Mavis Pittilla
Gordon Higginson
Estelle Roberts
Shirley Maclaine
Doris Stokes

We all owe such a great debt to those who pushed the
boundaries of acceptance and strived for excellence.

Acknowledgements

I am really grateful for permission from Roy Stemman to reproduce an extract from his book *Spirit Communication*, on page 23; Marilyn Pither, Nicola Howell and Carol Stirling for permission to print extracts from their descriptions of the trance demonstration, printed on pages 124–126; Tony Ortzen of *Psychic News* for his permission to use the extract from the article printed on page 141 and Jane Fryer, for permission to use an extract from her *Daily Express* article on pages 177–8.

I'd also like to thank Hilary and Craig Goldman of IPM and all the people I've worked with on all my television series, particularly *Psychic Detective and Legend Detectives*, whose experiences have given me so much fascinating and moving insight. I am so grateful to you all.

Thanks to Vivienne Foster and the tour company for giving me such a great opportunity to reach a wider audience, to Barbara and to everyone at Hodder for their support.

Finally, my utmost gratitude to Stuart for his invaluable help whilst writing this book and continued support of my work.

Contents

Introduction

Mankind, it is said, rarely escapes his or her destiny, but I must confess that, as far back as I can remember, I *never* wanted to escape mine. On the contrary, I have always been thrilled with my lot! Without wishing to sound pompous or, in any way, full of my own self-importance, I can only tell how it *was* – and *is* – for me.

From babyhood, when I discovered that I was able to come out of my body, take flight and float freely around our house and still be with my parents when they thought I was in my cot fast asleep, I always felt different, was always aware that I was seeing, hearing, feeling and sensing things that were beyond the ken, so to speak, of those who shared my life. But none of this troubled me. On the contrary, I took to the paranormal like the proverbial duck takes to water!

From that time onwards, my life contained some extraordinary out-of-body experiences and, as I progressed into childhood, there were several meetings with spirits, which incidentally never alarmed or scared me. Even at that young age, although I could not have put it into words, I felt I was a man of destiny; *blessed* to have been given such a gift. Convinced, though, that my schoolfriends would think I was an oddball – mad as a hatter – I soon learned to keep these other-worldly experiences to myself! From the age of sixteen, however, I knew, without a shadow of a doubt, that I was *destined* to use my paranormal powers by becoming a medium, and I began this work by giving readings and conducting séances and healing sessions in halls, churches and people's homes.

So it was that, determined to be the architect of my own good fortune and use the gifts I had been given, I served a long apprenticeship in these ways before becoming a full-time medium and teacher of psychic skills at colleges and spiritual centres all over Europe, and running regular seminars and workshops throughout the UK. It all seemed a far cry from being born in the East End of London in 1969, the son of a painter/decorator and a hairdresser, but I could not have had a happier time growing up in Canvey Island, Essex, and I was more than happy to be of service to the spirits and bring their messages to their loved ones.

In 2004, I was thrilled to discover that the transmission of my first television series, *Street Psychic*, had changed many people's beliefs about the afterlife. For this programme, I was asked to walk the streets of different towns and cities in the UK – and in San Francisco – stopping astonished passers-by and inviting them to have an instant one-to-one reading. Then, after *Street Psychic*, I made several other TV programmes including *Psychic School*, *The 3 Mediums* with Derek Acorah and Colin Fry, *Psychic Detective* – and I also appeared on Colin's TV programme, *6ixth Sense*.

One way or another, the year 2004 was a pretty amazing year for me, one in which I was able to draw on all my psychic skills and mediumship. I enjoyed every moment of it. In particular, the 'In High Spirits Tour 2004' was one of the biggest undertakings of the year and one of the things that left a lasting impression on me. When I was finalising the dates for this show with my tour manager, Vivienne Foster, I remember thinking what a mammoth undertaking it was going to be, but I never fully realised the impact it would have on me. When I was offered this tour, I felt *very* excited and *very* humble. For a start, I could hardly believe that others thought I was worthy of being given such an opportunity, and I felt a massive weight of responsibility on my shoulders. The knowledge that so many thousands of people would be coming to see me and would be pinning their hopes on me bringing messages from their loved ones was very daunting, but that made me even more determined to be on form every single night so that I could be of service to them and the spirit world.

Although I believe myself to be one of the luckiest mediums in the world and I thoroughly appreciate all the opportunities and challenges my work brings me, I do not mind admitting that I do feel the pressure sometimes. If I have learned one thing in the past twelve months of touring, it is coming to the understanding that there is so much grief, pain and anguish in every town up and down the country, resulting in an immense need in the people I demonstrate for. Each night before I go on stage, I pray that I will be the best vehicle I can to bring messages through from the spirit world, a wondrous place of unlimited possibilities where those who have grown old and wizened are able to regain their looks and youth, where those who were sick and lame are made well and whole again, and where, one day, we will all be reunited with those we hold most dear.

I categorise myself as a clairsentient – somebody who is able to sense and feel the other world – and I have two main spirit guides who help me in my work. One is Zintar, who is a very ancient Tibetan monk. The other I simply know by his name, which is Star. I have never seen Star because, up until now, he has not chosen to show himself to me. Over the years I have only ever perceived him as a pure white light. These two spirits are wonderful heavenly beings who work with me – and through me – and help me to bring messages from the other world. They also, in some difficult-to-explain mystical way, look after me.

Whatever the coming years hold for me, whether it is more one-to-one readings in small venues or people's homes, or tours and TV series, you can bet I will enjoy every single minute of it. One thing's for sure, for as long as there are people out there who want to listen, I will be there, fulfilling my destiny and shouting the simple truth from the rooftops – a truth I have known since early childhood – *'We cannot die. Physical death is just the next part of our fantastic journey!'*

So, whatever *your* thoughts on the afterlife – and whether such considerations just touch you for a moment or change your entire outlook for the rest of your life – I would love to say: *'Welcome to my world and the world of spirit – it's okay to be a believer'* and you can feel proud to be a member of this ever-growing club.

What I find *really* fascinating about the new-found popularity and interest in the spirit world, is the opportunity it gives to us all to ponder on what knowing that we survive physical death does to our outlook on our day-to-day life and the way we handle the situations we find ourselves in. If we come to accept the existence of a spirit world because we have received – or witnessed – a fantastic message from a loved one, surely we must then accept that death is not the end of our life. And the natural progression of this is to accept that *this* life is just a minute part of our total infinite existence; and that when we die we leave behind all the embellishments that stand between us and our true selves. What we take with us, then, is the kernel of truth that lies at the heart of all faiths:

that we are truly 'chips' off the divine block and, therefore, *eternal*.

One of the most satisfying moments in my work is when somebody approaches me and says: 'When people lose a loved one, it feels like the end of the world. But through people like you, I now know we can reach back to them and know they are still around us, still looking out for us, and we are not alone.' That, then, is what I believe my destiny is about – bringing people to this moment of truth. And if this book achieves anything, I would like it to be the knowledge that we can go forward with a spring in our step and a twinkle in our eye knowing that life is an eternal process – *we cannot die* – and we are *always* watched over and guided by somebody somewhere.

It just remains for me to add that while you are reading this book, you will doubtless find yourself confronted with some extraordinary events and happenings that I can only ask you to take on trust while you continue on this journey with me. Some things within the pages of this book will defy logic, some will not be immediately evident to everyone, some may create a rollercoaster of emotions for some and some may present a real challenge for others. But, whatever you experience as you read on, I am hoping that you will allow yourself to remain open-minded and aware that the experiences are mine and those of people I have met and read and demonstrated for.

They are experiences that have changed my life – and it is my dearest hope that reading about them will change your life, too; or, at the very least, set you upon your own spiritual quest. Sometimes we go through life as if we are only partially sighted, and it is only when we are prepared to expand our vision – and take other people's experiences on trust – that our eyes are prised open wider and we can begin to reach out and touch and embrace eternity. I can hope for no better gift for you.

Tony Stockwell
Essex, 2005

I

We are Eternal

I would like to begin this chapter by saying that all of my work to date, not only on TV but the years I have spent developing my gifts of mediumship, has made me believe one hundred per cent that we are *eternal* beings; and that this belief, which on many occasions has shaken me to my very core, has affected the way I view life and death, and relationships in this world and the next. I can't remember a particular moment when this realisation came to me, when I embraced eternity for the very first time. I can only say that, as far back as I can remember, *that* conviction has always been with me. There was no great revelation, no thunder and lightning, just a calm quiet acceptance and certainty that we do not die, and that this moment now is but *one* stage in our existence.

Paranormal experiences must have come to me from a very early age because, even now, I can recall some extraordinary events that occurred during my childhood. The following is one example.

As the younger of two children growing up in Canvey Island, I had the smallest bedroom in the house, which was rather an unusual shape because part of the stairwell was situated within it. As this shape made it impossible to fit a wardrobe and a bed into the room, my dad, who could turn his hand to anything, constructed a bunk bed for me that had a little wooden ladder for climbing in and out of it, and a large storage cupboard underneath which could be used as a play-den and somewhere to store my toys and other treasures. From

7

about the age of six, often as I got into that bed, extraordinary things began to happen; and, bizarre though it may seem, I became desperate for my parents to buy me a red-and-gold beaded curtain that could be hung from the ceiling to act as a kind of exotic screen that would enclose my bunk bed, and enable me to peer through into the room. As I had never set eyes on such an object, this was an extraordinary obsession in itself and, if asked, I honestly could not have explained *why* I wanted such a thing. In the event, although I never actually acquired the screen, the image of it still existed in my mind's eye when I was lying in bed and the sheets, covers and pillows also transformed themselves from cotton into a very exotic brightly-coloured silk material!

One day, when I awoke from a very deep sleep, I felt my bed rocking and, as I held on to both sides of the mattress to steady myself, the bed began to sway from side to side. I wasn't in the least bit frightened. On the contrary, I remember closing my eyes and squealing with excitement as it suddenly dawned on me that I was sitting, like a young rajah or sultan, in a decorative carry-chair perched on the back of an elephant. Thrilled to bits, I felt myself being carried along a street somewhere in India that was bustling with half-naked people, who, as part of a procession, were accompanying me seated on top of the elephant. This imagery did not happen on only one occasion. It occurred several times when I was between the ages of six and nine and, each time, I found it so fascinating that I actually learned how to re-evoke this event when I climbed into my bunk bed.

I've never really tried to explain this childhood experience but, if pressed now, I would say that I was re-living an event from one of my previous lives – an event that had been *so* special and *so* exciting at the time that it had become indelibly imprinted on my memory.

Round about the same time, I remember having another paranormal experience in my bedroom which, on this occasion, took place in the playden that my dad had built for me under the bed. One night when I was lying in my bunk, I heard a voice calling my name. Now this, in itself, was nothing unusual. I often heard my name being called during my childhood and I often got on everybody's nerves, my family's and my friends', by constantly going up to them and saying: 'Yes? What do you want?'

'Nothing,' they would reply. 'I didn't call you.'

'Well, *somebody* did,' I would answer back, peeved.

On the name-calling occasion in my bedroom, though, I was aware that it was a voice I had never heard before, an unusual high-pitched, sing-song kind of voice that seemed to be coming from beneath my bed; and it was calling: '*T-o-n-y* . . . T-o-n-y . . .'

'What do you want?' I asked, peering over the edge of my bunk, and realising that the voice was definitely emanating from inside my playden. But the voice just continued, sing-song fashion, to call my name.

Climbing out of bed and going down to ground level, I opened the door to my den and peered in. Although I could still hear the little voice whispering *T-o-n-y*, I couldn't see a thing. I wasn't frightened, though, and I didn't even hesitate before I climbed inside. As I did so and as my eyes became accustomed to the gloom within, I saw the outline of a little boy, crouched in the far corner, who was of a similar age to me. His face, I noticed, was exceedingly dirty and his clothes really scruffy.

'You look as if you've been dragged through a hedge backwards,' I said, repeating something my mum was fond of saying.

''Ello mate,' he said in what was definitely an East End London accent. ''Ow are yuh?'

'Fine,' I replied, thinking he sounded like a grown-up. 'How are you?'

And there we sat, the little ragamuffin and me, like two little old men, exchanging the time of day and getting to know each other; and all the while I was trying to work out *how* and *why* he had come to be in *my* playden, *my* toy cupboard.

I can't remember now how long we stayed there that first time or what we talked about, but I do remember him telling me his name was Arthur, and that, as he was an orphan and had had nowhere to lay his head, he had 'died of the cold'.

'Dyin' was nice,' he said. 'Just like bein' wrapped up in a lovely warm blanket.'

Apart from that remark, all our conversations were pretty straightforward and that continued to be the case when he reappeared on four other occasions before disappearing again from my life. Right up until now, his presence in my playden remains a bit of a riddle and I don't know *why* he sought me out. Maybe it was simply because he knew that *I* would be able to hear and see him, and wanting somebody of his own age to play with was sufficient reason for him to put in those appearances. He is certainly not somebody who has, as yet, crossed my path again, so I am inclined to believe that, although he is part of my soul group, we may not meet again in this lifetime and we may have to wait a while longer before we are reunited.

One very curious thing about those meetings, though, is that, although my mum always sent me off to bed freshly bathed and squeaky-clean, there was always a shock in store for her in the morning. Each time after my ragamuffin spirit had put in one of his appearances, she would look at my face and exclaim in horrified tones: 'What on earth have you been doing with yourself? How did you get such a dirty face?'

When, having shrugged my shoulders, I stood on my tiptoes

to look in the mirror, I could see what she meant. My face was that of a street urchin's or chimney-sweep's boy, every bit as grubby as my little visitor's had been!

Once we accept that life is eternal, our existence is turned upside down. We view everything in a different *long-term*, as opposed to *short-term*, way and at a very profound level this affects how we choose to live each day, how we interact with others, how we treat our family, colleagues, neighbours and strangers, and how we deal with joy and sorrow, gain and loss, grief and mourning. Everything – and I do mean *everything* – takes on a whole new meaning. This is because there is a wealth of difference between believing we only need to look after number one and make the best of this life of 'three score years and ten', and realising that all the joys and the sorrows do not end there; that there is more – *and yet more* – to come; and that how we live and how we treat others has a far-reaching effect on the whole!

Embracing eternity is rather like looking at a vast vista of plains and valleys, hills and mountains, on and beyond, as far as the eye can see. Some things we see close-up, others at a distance, and others, however much we may strain our eyes, are out of vision. But not being able to see the whole vista, on demand, all at once, does not mean it is *not* there or does *not* exist. It simply means we have to make an effort, take the first step and start walking if we want to see the rest!

The beauty of reflecting on these things today is that there are now so many opportunities available to increase our knowledge of other-worldly matters! There is no doubt, for example, that over the past couple of years the work of mediums and psychics has spread from churches and halls into our homes. And, largely thanks to LIVINGtv in the UK, with its programmes like *6ixth Sense* and *Street Psychic*, and also the hugely popular American shows *Crossing Over* with John Edward and *Beyond* with James Van Praagh, now so many more people on the planet who are lucky enough to have access to a television can now see mediums at work on almost a daily basis.

The traditional image, then, of a medium sitting at a table in a dimly lit room, calling out in a spooky voice, 'Is there anybody there?' in the hope that a spirit will respond, is one that you are now only likely to come across in old black-and-white classic films. Today, far from this being the case, mediums can communicate with spirits while standing on stage within the blinding arc of a spotlight, or by being beamed by TV satellite to millions around the world.

Television, then, has introduced the possibility that there is life after death, and that we are able to communicate with our loved ones, to many people who would not have dreamed of going to a Spiritualist meeting. Today, however, they can reflect on questions such as 'Is it *really* possible to communicate with loved ones after they have passed over?' without even getting out of their armchairs!

I must add, though, that while I am delighted to be working on television, I am equally happy demonstrating mediumship in people's homes and working in Spiritualist churches and development groups. In other words I am only too happy to try to lift the veil between our world and the next *anywhere*.

Although television has brought mediumship into the spotlight and attracted the attention of a new generation, it is important to remember it is not just there for entertainment. Communicating with the spirit world is one of the foundations of the Spiritualist religion and for many people it is not just a belief, it is a way of life. It is about bringing evidence from those we love who have gone home before us that we survive death; and that all the great teachers and philosophers – and their work – remain forever available for us to share in the amazing insights they have to offer on the purpose of our existence. It is truly wonderful to appreciate that no learning is lost and that all the great teachings can still enhance our lives in the moment now.

Likewise, mediumship is not something that has come into existence in recent years. It has been around forever! Many people, for example, regard Jesus as one of the greatest mediums who was in touch with this world and the next, and able to practise spiritual healing and channel through to us one of the most life-enhancing philosophies of all time. Not only did he believe in Spirit, he *lived* it.

Since that time, there have been many pioneering mediums who have dedicated their lives to a higher purpose and who have paved the way for mediums, such as myself, Colin Fry, and John Edward to work in public arenas and, on the whole, to be accepted.

Many of the great mediums of times gone by have inspired me in my work. Among these are Doris Stokes, Estelle Roberts, Minnie Harrison and Gordon Higginson to name but a few. All were brave pioneers who extended the boundaries of our work, raised the quality of mediumship and proved beyond any doubt that we can connect with the spirit world – that it is as real as you and me, and that death is just like stepping into the next room.

The actual lifting of the veil between the two worlds, though, is not always easy. There is, I have discovered over the years, a muzziness around the earth's atmosphere which is created by mankind's madness: the terrible materialism that exists in so many places, the frenetic pace at which so many of us have chosen to live, and the dreadful acts of violence and grief that are daily occurrences in our world. But when we make the effort to rise above all this and listen to each other and blend with the other world, it is as if we create a ray of light that can penetrate and shine through the veil of darkness that divides us; and when those in the other world glimpse that light, which may only last a couple of minutes, they are able to tune into that energy and break through the veil and communicate with us.

At such times, we mediums mainly draw on the gift of clairvoyance, clairaudience or clairsentience, or maybe a combination of all of these, to help us communicate with the spirit world. These three words – clairvoyance, clairaudience and clairsentience – which originate in the French language, mean clear seeing, clear hearing and clear sensing. The clairvoyant faculty allows a medium to *see* images and symbols; clairaudience allows him or her to *hear* sounds and the words of the spirits, such as a person's name being spoken; and clairsentience allows us to *sense – feel –* the spirits' presence. Sometimes clairsentience is more like clair-knowing. The information is just there in your mind. You know it to be true, but you have no knowledge of how it got there. You know, for example, how old a person was when they passed, the circumstances of their passing, and who they now wish to connect with.

It is not enough, however, just to see clairvoyantly, hear clairaudiently or sense clairsentiently. We also have to interpret what we are seeing, hearing and feeling. The work of a medium, then, is exactly what the word itself implies: to act as an *intermediary* – an intermediary between those who have passed on and those who are still in this world.

Many mediums claim that one of the gifts – clairvoyance, clairaudience or clairsentience – is predominant in their work, and they describe themselves either as a clairvoyant, clairaudient or clairsentient. I am lucky. Although I am predominantly a clairsentient, I am actually blessed by being able to draw on all three.

The way I experience spirit communication is, initially, by receiving an almost overwhelming sense of the presence of the other world. Then, in a moment, I can feel whether it is the spirit of a man or woman or child who has come alongside me and is trying to connect with me. Information then begins to come through. I can then, for example, *feel* the age the person was when they passed. I also know if they passed with a medical condition and if they are now looking for a loved one somewhere within the audience. At times, all these impressions come to me in a flash and sometimes they are accompanied by a clear visual image. I can *see*, for example, the colour of the person's eyes, or the colour of a lady's dress, or the favourite shade of nail varnish that she used throughout her life. Then, on a good day, I am also able to *hear* words, just as clearly from the other world as I can from the living world. Usually it is a name of a person or a place name. In other words, I can *feel*, *see* and *hear* the spirit, who is connecting with me from the other side, in order to communicate with a loved one on this side.

An incident that will illustrate clairaudience occurred just a few weeks ago. Having been invited to take a small seminar in Sweden, I left home very early to catch a plane from Stansted Airport. I'm never at my best first thing and, as I'd also been working flat-out for several weeks, I kept my eyes firmly closed in the taxi on the way to the airport so that I would not have to enter into conversation with the taxi driver. Needless to say, the flight was delayed and by the time I took my seat on the plane, I was feeling, along with all the other passengers, very tired and frayed at the edges. Then, just as I slipped into a comfortable doze, I was awakened by one of the cabin crew asking me if I wanted anything from the trolley.

'Twenty-four hours' sleep!' was my first thought, but I settled for a cup of tea!

Moments later, as I sat there sipping the tea, an incredible transformation came over me. Outside the window, the sun was just rising and God, the creator, was at his/her best, painting all the clouds pink and rimming them with an orange or purple glow. Filled with awe at the sheer beauty of creation, I became increasingly refreshed and elated as I witnessed the coming of the new dawn.

'*Dawn*! That's *my* name,' a lady's voice said from the seat alongside me. But when I looked round, there wasn't a lady, just a middle-aged man reading a newspaper.

'He's my husband,' the voice announced, proudly. 'His name is Roger.'

In my elated state, it took a moment for me to realise what was going on. I was receiving clairaudience from the spirit world. She was speaking, I could hear her and, what's more I was hearing the voice even clearer than I had heard other voices of late.

As my heart began to race from fear of spoiling the connection, I said gently and silently under my breath: 'Okay, Dawn, I can hear you, can you hear me?'

For a moment there was no reply and I thought I had lost her, but then the voice repeated: 'That's my Roger. *Please* tell him I'm here'.

Now that was a tall order! I am used to bringing messages to people from the spirit world, but I do not usually approach complete strangers and tell them things they may not want to hear, things that may scare or alarm them. But Dawn's voice was so insistent, I felt I had to do something.

Turning to the man at my side, I said, hoping he would not notice I was wearing a watch: 'Could you possibly tell me the time, please?'

His response, having consulted his watch, was to tell me the time without making any eye contact whatsoever.

'What now?' I thought, as Dawn began to urge me on again.

'Have you been to Sweden before?' I asked politely.

'A couple of times,' he replied equally politely, not looking up from his paper.

'How do you feel about flying?'

I knew I was behaving like an irritating fly and that all he wanted to do was to sit there quietly and read.

'I'd rather drive,' he replied. 'But flying's a lot faster.'

Just as I was wondering where we could go from there, he folded up his newspaper in a resigned kind of way and, turning to me, said: 'My name's . . .'

I held my breath.

'Roger. What's yours?'

'Tony,' I replied, trying not to sound too stunned that he had said *Roger*!

After we had chatted for a while, I asked him what he did for a living, then he asked me what I did.

'I'm a medium,' I replied, looking him straight in the eye.

'Oh, Lord!' he said smirking and looking at me as if I had just landed from Mars. 'I don't believe in any of that, I'm afraid. You're *not* going to tell me you can see someone, other than yourself, sitting with me, are you?'

With Dawn's voice still resounding in my ear, I took a deep breath and said: 'D'you know a lady in the other world named Dawn?'

As the smirk on his face crumpled and faded, I knew that the replacement expression on his face was one that I would never forget.

'*That's* my wife's name,' he gasped. 'She died two weeks ago. I don't understand. I've never seen you before. You couldn't have known that?'

'I can hear her voice,' I said quietly. 'She's here with us in the plane and, if you will allow me, I can tell you what she's saying.'

He was obviously shaken and somewhat reluctant to agree, but he nodded just the same.

Closing my eyes, I focused on Dawn, then repeated what I heard: 'She's saying: "Send my love to Sarah and Ben and tell them I will always love them. Tell them . . ."'

Before I could finish the sentence, Roger broke down in tears.

'Sarah and Ben are our children,' he sobbed.

Dawn then told me her mother's and her brother's name and left a simple loving message for both of them. Just as I thought she was moving away from us, she added: 'Tell Roger I know he has my gloves in his pocket.'

When I passed this message on, Roger clicked open his seat belt, stumbled to his feet, reached in the overhead luggage compartment and pulled out his jacket. The moment he sat down again, he put his hand in his left pocket and, sobbing quietly, pulled out a pair of small black leather gloves.

He remained deep in thought for the rest of the journey, but I didn't interrupt him. Without asking, I could tell that he was feeling much calmer and much more at ease within himself. He didn't speak again until the plane had touched down and taxied to a standstill then, turning to me, he said: 'What can I say? What can I say other than *thank you* – and *bless you*!'

'That's more than enough,' I replied, smiling.

I have had many similar experiences, but that clairaudient connection, when the voice was so clear, still stands out in my mind. I am more used to *feeling* or *seeing* the spirits, so to *hear* Dawn's voice that clearly was a very special blessing. Maybe my mind had been lifted to another level by the incredible beauty of the new dawn; or maybe Dawn was just very determined to get through to Roger. Either way that connection, spontaneous and simple as it was, left me feeling on top of the world and honoured to be chosen for the work that I do.

Like every other living person, of course, we mediums cannot spend all our time feeling on top of the world! We also have to live and function in everyday life, but by attending development classes and seminars we have learned a unique and wonderful knack of raising and shifting our energy and awareness, so that we are able to lift the veil between the two worlds and communicate with the spirit world. Being sensitive to others and to your surroundings is obviously an essential aspect of mediumship. And, in the early days, as our sensitivity becomes more and more heightened through the work, it is very important to ensure that things do not get out of proportion or perspective. One fatal mistake is if the medium's ego comes into play and the belief creeps in that the messenger is more important than the message. Nothing blunts the sensitivities quicker than this! Likewise, no human being, however much they love their work, can work twenty-four hours a day. Learning to switch off and earth oneself by doing ordinary everyday things, such as watering the garden and walking the dog, is vital.

Mediums, if they are to give of their best, need to accept at an early stage that they are ordinary people who are blessed with an extraordinary gift; and that like everybody else, who gets the measure of their activities wrong and overdoes things, they can suffer burn-out. This is a sad state of affairs because if you are feeling below par, out of sorts, tired and stressed, the messages from the spirits are less clear, or even distorted. Burn-out is rather like forgetting to charge your mobile phone and then discovering it is running on a low battery just when you need it most!

There was an occasion during the summer of 2005, for example, when I experienced this. At the time I was very busy demonstrating in theatres up and down the country for my 'Best of British Mediumship' tour while, at the same time, filming two new television series – *Legend Detectives* for the Discovery Channel and *Psychic Detective* for LIVINGtv.

The latter programme, which involved some emotionally draining shoots, was particularly challenging. On one occasion, after I had been investigating the last moments of a murdered boy's life in order to help bring some closure for his parents, I clearly overtaxed my energies. On the drive home at the end of the day's filming, I suddenly felt drained to the point of exhaustion and, as my body began to tremble uncontrollably, I burst into tears. It was some moments before I realised I was suffering from burn-out. Fortunately, I have an excellent support network in my family and friends, who are always there to take care of me and to remind me that life is for living as well as for working. These are the moments when the simple things in life restore me to full health and vigour and allow me to continue with the work I so love doing.

The person or people I am reading for also play an important role in my work. If they are very sceptical or on the defensive and constantly putting up barriers, this can take its toll and be off-putting. If, on the other hand, they are willing to be open-minded and unbiased, a medium with the help of the spirits can merge this world and the next, and demonstrate that our loved ones have survived death and that their unique personality and individuality remain intact.

As for us mediums, when communication flows freely through us from the spirit world, we quite naturally experience an intense high, which sometimes can be followed by an equally intense low. In my experience, though, my energies are soon replenished and I never remain feeling low for long. After all, what could be better than using the gift of mediumship I have been given to bring comfort and hope to those who are in the depths of despair that bereavement can bring. Each time I see the light creeping back into a person's eyes and see their spirits begin to lift as they receive a life-enhancing confirmation that their loved one lives on and there is life after death, my heart soars. Then I am more than ready for another day in my chosen work.

Thanks, then, to the huge exposure given to the paranormal by today's media, we are now living in a time when it is much more acceptable to be a believer, and okay to tell our friends we have consulted a medium. We will certainly not get the strange glances our parents, grandparents and great grandparents would doubtless have encountered had they been so open about their visits to those 'spooky people who talk to the dead'. In their day there were even many instances of psychics and mediums being jailed for using their gifts.

In the history of Spiritualism, for example, we have our very own martyr. Her name was Helen Duncan and she was described as a Scottish Spiritualist Materialisation medium – and a housewife – through whose body ectoplasm flowed and formed itself into human figures which could walk and talk and greet their living relatives with the kind of intimate information that was known only within their families.

A renowned psychic, Helen found herself caught up in the centre of a Second World War legal battle, which ended with her conviction for a crime under Britain's ancient Witchcraft Act.

All this came about when, during a séance, Helen informed a mother that her young sailor son was dead.

'No – *no*,' the lady protested. 'My son is *alive*.'

Helen then materialised the form of a sailor with the name

HMS *Barham* on his cap, and the boy appeared and told his mother that he had 'gone down the day before on HMS *Barham*'.

Later, when the grief-stricken mother contacted the War Office and told them she had information that HMS *Barham* had gone down with all hands lost, Helen found herself in serious trouble.

Having initially denied that HMS *Barham* had been sunk, the English government had Helen arrested as a spy. Then, when her information was proven to be correct, she was charged as a witch and jailed for nine months. It was only because of this case that the Witchcraft Act was repealed and mediums were allowed to act as freely and openly as they do today.

Since those days Helen, who died in 1956, has been remembered as the 'victim of the last witch trial' and as a 'martyr for Spiritualism'. The British Society of Paranormal Studies, which refers to her as a 'beacon of light that lets her honour and leadership shine through a fog of doubts and fears', has embarked on legal efforts to have her granted a posthumous pardon.

The change in the acceptance of psychics and mediums since Helen's days has been absolutely incredible and, even as a psychic I can say, 'I didn't see *that* coming!'

Personally I have never been one to bother myself with the sceptics of this world. As far as I am concerned that's their path and this is mine. If they don't believe in the work I do – and think we are all charlatans – who am I to challenge or attempt to change their opinion?

Having said that, nobody is more delighted than I am when somebody who has arrived in a stroppy, belligerent mood, goes away a changed person or, at least, a person who has been given food for thought. Thanks to the spirits, this has often been the case: the offering of a loved one's name when the person has been least expecting it or the mention of a particularly intimate characteristic or event, known only to the family, can shake the ground beneath their feet!

These days, however, whenever I come face-to-face with a particularly difficult sceptic who would not, in his or her words, change their views for 'all the tea in China', I take comfort in the following paragraphs that Roy Stemman, a writer and journalist who has specialised in the field of the paranormal for over forty years, wrote about me in his book *Spirit Communication*:

It is Tony Stockwell's approach that, in my opinion, has been the most refreshing and evidential . . . I attended one of his demonstrations at the New Theatre in Oxford in May 2004, and was impressed on several counts. Although there were more females than males in the audience – which is also typical of Spiritualist churches – their ages ranged from teens to eighties. Very few, I suspect, knew where the nearest Spiritualist church was or had even considered visiting it; but the prospect of communicating with the next world in the comfort of a modern theatre was irresistible . . . Sharing the platform with Stockwell was a video camera pointed at the audience. When he singled out an individual to receive a spirit message, the camera zoomed in and the image it captured was displayed on a large screen behind the medium. The recipients were also handed a microphone so that everyone in the theatre could hear their responses. It's a far cry from the early days of Spiritualism and will not be to everyone's liking, but it is certainly breathing new life into the gift of mediumship and opening minds to the possibility of spirit communication.

I find the thought that I, along with other high profile mediums like Colin Fry and John Edward, may be 'breathing new life into the gift of mediumship' a deeply satisfying one. And I regard 'opening minds to the possibility of spirit communication' a vital part of my vocation; one that I hold in mind every day before I start work. But what I most want to stress here is that this opening up to the realisation that we are eternal is only the *first* step on the journey. Once we have connected with that realisation, our existence, as I mentioned in the Introduction to this book, is turned upside down, and we begin to view everything in a different way, including how we interact with others on a daily basis, how our relationships develop and deepen, and how we deal with grief and the loss of our loved ones.

This life, in other words, will never be the same again; and, just like me, you will discover that the belief in an afterlife will shake you to the very depths of your being, and the way you view this life and the death that brings it to a temporary close will be transformed.

From experience, I can confirm that accepting that we are all *eternal* beings opens up door after door and sets into motion trains of thought and questions that may take us an eternity to discover all the answers. Our only comfort is that *every* journey, however long or short, begins with just one step – and what I would love readers of this book to do most of all is to open up their minds to the possibility of taking that first step so that they can begin the walk that will eventually enable them to embrace eternity!

2
Rising to the Challenge

When I began working with spirits and passing on their messages, I did not, in my wildest dreams, foresee all that they would come to mean to me, or all the places my work would take me to or the new challenges I would need to face on a daily basis. *That* may surprise some people who believe that we psychics know everything and can predict events in our own lives, including how to avoid traffic that has become gridlocked a few miles down the road! But that is *not* how it works. Our psychic and mediumistic gifts are given and used and developed for the spirits that we serve and, through them, for the benefit of others. When I am working and completely focused on other-worldly matters, my psychic gifts are to hand; when I am not working and I am just going about ordinary everyday life, I find myself in traffic jams or waiting for a train that has been cancelled like everybody else.

Over the years, some of the ways in which I work have changed, and to ensure that I am able to do my best for the spirits and for those who are hoping for messages from their loved ones, I always take care to detach myself from everyday events and prepare for the different sessions. I may do this by meditating or by emptying my mind and bringing myself into the present with some simple breathing or visualisation exercises.

Having got myself into the right frame of mind, I could say that *all* my work, whether it is spent giving one-to-one readings, demonstrating on stage in front of thousands of people, or taking a seminar for an eager group of students, is a challenge – and *that* would be true. But, as in all walks of life, some challenges prove to be more of a challenge than others – mega challenges in fact!

This was the case in 2004 when I was involved in making the pilot episode of *Psychic Detective* for LIVINGtv. A totally different approach from any of my previous psychic work was needed for this and, not surprisingly given its subject matter, it proved to be a somewhat challenging, roller-coaster emotional journey. In the event, though, the pilot proved to be such a success with the powers-that-be that they asked me to do another six episodes.

I must confess I had some very strong reservations about taking on this particular challenge. However professional you are, it is almost impossible to remain completely emotionally detached when working on cases where families are hoping for answers to the death or mysterious disappearance of a loved one.

There was also another dilemma. I had insisted that I only wanted to work on cases where the investigations would not open up old wounds that had already started to heal, but how could I be sure of this when I had also insisted that I did not want to be told any details of the investigation before we started filming?

After much deliberation and soul-searching, I decided to trust IPM, the producers of the show and also the makers of *Street Psychic* and *6ixth Sense*, to act as an intermediary and only put forward cases where there was a possibility that some healing or closure could be gained for the family involved. I also felt reassured by the fact that it was the families who had, either directly or indirectly, approached the makers of the programme, rather than the other way round!

The format for each of the programmes, then and now, was

the same. They began with a one-to-one reading for a person or couple who had a story to tell, a mystery to unravel or a situation that had left many unanswered questions. The TV production team brought these people to a beautiful penthouse apartment, with stunning views over London. There we met for the first time and, after the initial greetings, the reading began.

I started each *Psychic Detective* as a blank canvas. I had no advance knowledge of why people were there and what they hoped to establish and, therefore, no preconceived ideas. In doing this I realised I was placing myself in a precarious position. If I failed to bring information through from the spirit world, I would be judged a failure; and if I succeeded in making a good link and providing new evidence, a certain section of the population would think I had been forearmed with the facts of the case. It could prove to be a no-win situation. In the end, however, I decided to put all these doubts aside and do what I could to the best of my abilities.

I was, of course, very familiar with giving one-to-one readings, but these particular consultations were concerned with mostly tragic, heartbreaking events. Although I have never become blasé about listening to people expressing their pain and sorrow, and I never take grief for granted, the fact that there was such a strong element of the unknown in regards to how people came to pass on in the *Psychic Detective* series, obviously made matters much more difficult than usual.

When we lose a loved one, it is natural to want *all* the answers, and, when we get them, this helps to bring about closure and allows us to move on with our life. In most of the *Psychic Detective* cases, however, this was not what had happened. There were so many unanswered questions and half-truths that the mourners were left imprisoned in time and space by the loss of the person.

In all, for the series I read for eight people (or couples), six of whom would eventually be used as part of the investigations. Thanks to the spirits, the majority of the readings went very well, and were full of wonderfully accurate pieces of information. This is because when spirits have a great need to be heard, their connections are so much clearer. It is as if their need to come back and tell their story – and thus prove that their spirit has survived – combines with the need of the people I am reading for. This, in turn, allows me an extra special clarity of mediumship which enables me to pass on the most intricate information from beyond the grave.

Imagine, then, my delight when each of the people, some of whom had travelled hundreds of miles for their reading, did receive a degree of closure. Each case was as unique and as challenging as the last, but all had one common link: a terrible out-of-the-blue tragedy that had left unanswered questions surrounding the death of their loved one.

The first reading I did for the pilot episode was for Marie McCourt who asked for help in tracing the final resting place of her twenty-two-year-old daughter Helen, an insurance clerk in Liverpool who was murdered when she was walking home on a blustery, rain-lashed night in 1988.

Despite two thousand villagers turning out for a grim, inch-by-inch search, Helen's body had never been found. And, in the seventeen years that had passed since then, Marie had spent her weekends draining ponds and canals, clearing mine-shafts and claypits, searching hedgerows and digging up fields in a frantic search for her daughter's final resting place. Each Saturday she and her family would set off full of hope from their home in Billenge, near Wigan, clutching spades, metal detectors, strimmers and bundles of plastic police tape, hoping that this would be the day their torment of not knowing where Helen lay would come to an end. Although Helen's killer was jailed in 1989 – and is still behind bars – he had never responded to any of the family's anguished entreaties to reveal where he had placed his victim's body.

Marie's request for help had coincided with the commission of the pilot for *Psychic Detective*, and the production company and Marie McCourt knew that if they could feature this particular case, it would receive the publicity that was needed to place it firmly back in the public's mind. It was hoped that fresh leads would come to light.

The family had had to search in places where no one would want to go – in dirty, filthy sewers and mineshafts – looking for their beloved daughter. They told me that they felt it was a basic human right to bury your loved ones, to give them a proper, dignified burial and, understandably, they wanted their daughter in sacred ground, somewhere they could lay flowers and know she was beneath the headstone.

I was aware that if I were to have any hope of helping Marie I would need to visit her in her home and link with her energy and pray that I could make a connection with Helen. So, early one morning, I travelled to the small village where the family lived.

'I'm like a transmitter,' I remember explaining to Jane Fryer who was covering the event for the *Daily Express*. 'A medium is the link between the two worlds. I filter through thoughts and feelings, inspiration and information from those who have passed over. We're not dealing with an exact science here. I'm working with emotions, thoughts and feelings.'

All I really knew that day was that I was there to help a grieving mother locate her daughter's body and I began by asking Marie not to tell me anything else because with private readings – in which I sit with a person and try to connect with a loved one who has passed over – knowledge can often be a hindrance rather than a help.

I read for Marie for about an hour and gave her as much feedback as I could about Helen and, more importantly, about her passing. I never cease to be amazed by the power of the spirit, and as I sat holding pieces of Helen's jewellery, surrounded by dozens of photographs of her, she came through to me loud and clear.

'Helen was a very fun-loving and carefree girl, always laughing and had only kind words for those around her,' I said to Marie who totally agreed with this description.

Later, at the George and Dragon, the pub where the police investigation had proved that Helen was murdered by the landlord, I focused my attentions on an upstairs function room where there was a cold sinister energy. My heart began to race as I peeled back the memories of everything that happened in that unhappy place, and I had a very real sense that I was living through Helen's final moments.

'*Show* me Helen, *show* me,' I kept repeating, and I evoked everything I had learned – her age and personality – so I could travel back in time.

Then, as my mind began to fill with images, I became acutely aware of Helen's last moments. I could feel her being dragged upstairs. Throughout this time, I felt myself walking Helen's last footsteps; and, with the help of my spirit guides, Zintar and Star, the moment of her passing over and her release and the exact spot where she dropped to the ground was revealed to me.

I was also aware that there were clues that Helen was desperately trying to convey to me.

Then, while I was still reeling from all this, I received one of the most powerful visions I had ever had and I knew that the image of a place that had entered my mind held the key to where Helen would eventually be found. The scene I saw was of a mound-like hill, topped by four smallish trees.

Immediately beneath the hill was a gravel area, and to the left of this a thicket with brambles. In the foreground was a winding path or lane that ran past a dilapidated, desolate stone house and then on to a gravel area. I was also aware of water running nearby.

Armed with this vision still strong in my mind, I travelled to South Wales to meet up with a computer graphics expert, and there in his studio we spent most of the day constructing a physical representation of the image I had seen. This picture was to become a major factor in the case, as local newspapers in Wigan joined in the search and asked their readers if they recognised the location shown in my vision. And that's what happened. Dozens of calls were received, many of which pinpointed a place that was about three miles from the pub.

During the filming we visited many of the places mentioned by members of the public and, although some had similar characteristics, none of them was the one I had been shown. This, as you can imagine, was very frustrating. I so wanted to do my best in helping to build up the picture of Helen's last resting place; but it was more important for me to be honest with Marie McCourt and remain true to the memory of her daughter, Helen, than to have a dramatic ending to *Psychic Detective*.

As the light was fading on the last day of filming, we had one last location to visit as the result of a single tip-off from somebody who had seen the picture in the paper. As we approached the area, all of us exhausted emotionally and physically, we came to an abrupt halt as the vision, which had sent shivers up my spine, came into sight.

It was the *exact* place I had seen in my vision, and it *exactly* matched our recreation of it. We subsequently learned that the stone house in the foreground was derelict at the time Helen died.

I sincerely believe that Helen McCourt from the other side had shown me the place that was important to her very last moments on earth; and I know this place has some part in the tragic murder of this beautiful young girl whose life was taken from her in her prime of life. Much of what I had told Marie about her daughter's final hours had tallied with the forensic evidence – the struggle in the pub, her final moments and then her being taken away in the boot of a car.

The headline in the next day's *Daily Express* read: HAS THE PSYCHIC DETECTIVE FOUND MY DAUGHTER? *Tony Stockwell's astonishing powers may finally bring to an end a 17-year-old mystery*. Another headline in the *Wigan Reporter* read PSY-CHIC COULD HOLD THE KEY TO McCOURT MYSTERY.

I do hope so, not for my sake, but because finding Helen's last resting place would bring such peace of mind to Marie and the rest of the McCourt family. They would no longer need to suffer the agony of not knowing where Helen lies, or need to endure the awful agitation engendered from being aware that Helen is still out there somewhere, or experience a sickening lurch in their stomachs every time another body is found. For this reason, although the *Psychic Detective* programme has now been transmitted, I am hoping to continue working with the McCourt family – and praying that my spirit guides will help me to put their minds at rest.

Just as I had anticipated, the new challenge had proved to be an emotional roller-coaster for everyone concerned with the making of the films, but the results were such that I felt comfortable about continuing with the series.

3
Goodbye for Now

One way and another, facing up to new challenges while working on *Psychic Detective* certainly drove home for me the fact that, given we are on this earth for such a short time, we should cherish every single moment and recognise this life for what it is: a time-allotted learning experience. One of the cases that helped me to appreciate this while working on the series was that of Stephen who was hoping for some answers concerning the life and death of Hannah Tailford.

A blond man in his forties, Stephen sat down in front of me with such pain etched on his features that I just knew the spirit people would want to help me help him.

Stephen, it turned out, was adopted at birth and knew nothing of his natural mother until an unexpected event, involving newspaper reporters, occurred when he was seven years old and changed his life forever.

Armed only with the name Stephen Tailford and completely unaware of their target's age, some reporters had called at his home to get his reaction to some news about his mother, a woman he did not even know existed.

'That's what brought everything to a head,' Stephen explained to me. 'When the newspaper chaps started knocking at the door of my adopted parents' home saying: "Can we speak to Stephen Tailford?" My parents' reply, as they tried to protect me from the terrible news about my birth mother, was: "There's nobody of *that* name living here." Nevertheless, after the reporters had gone, they realised that the moment had come when they had better tell me the history of who I really was.'

Now, forty years later, married and with a family of his own, Stephen's desire to find out more about his past and the reason why he had been given up for adoption, had led him to come to see me and take part in *Psychic Detective*.

Having insisted, as usual, on being kept completely in the dark at that stage, I knew nothing about Hannah Tailford, Stephen's mother, or why he had come to see me.

When we were sitting facing each other, I closed my eyes and tuned into the spirit world. Moments later, my eyes still tightly closed, I said: 'I have a lady here with me now who I believe to be your mother.'

Pausing and opening my eyes, I added: 'Is that correct? Is your mother in the spirit world.'

'Yes,' Stephen replied, his voice barely audible. 'Yes, she is.'

'I don't feel she passed recently,' I said. 'In fact, I'm getting the sense that she has been long-gone into the spirit world and that you were either *very* young when she passed or already disconnected in some way at that time. Is that true?'

'Yes, it is,' Stephen replied, not meeting my eyes.

'I feel that part of the reason you have come here today is to get some kind of clarification – an explanation – of what happened between you and your mother. I'm picking up on a sense of . . .' I paused, not quite sure for a moment, then I added: '*Betrayal* and a sense of *abandonment*.'

'Your mother is making it very clear to me that she wishes to apologise to you today,' I said gently. 'And she wants you to know that you are still her little boy and you will always be her little boy. This lady, like so many of us,' I added, as I noticed tears beginning to well up in Stephen's eyes, 'admits that she got some things *very* wrong in her life and she wants to make up for this, especially the things that concern you.' I paused, looking across at Stephen, as he sat there trying to keep his emotions under control. 'You know,' I continued gently, 'your mother's presence is strong, but I'm not getting any kind of connection to your dad. It's just as if he was never on the scene. Is that correct?'

'Yes, it is,' Stephen replied, finding the strength to look up and meet my eyes.

'Did you know that, in all, there were four children born to your mum – that you were *one* of four?'

'No!' Stephen replied startled, shaking his head. It was obvious from the expression on his face that he was deeply shocked by this news.

'Right now your mum is wanting to include your grandma – her mum – in the conversation,' I said, adding: 'Do you know if your grandma was called Annie?'

'No,' Stephen replied, shaking his head. 'I've no idea what my grandmother was called.'

'Well, maybe,' I said smiling, 'that could be investigated further. I'm certainly getting a very strong feeling of love from this lady.

'Have you ever had any links with the Newcastle area?' I continued.

'I don't actually know the name of the town or village,' Stephen replied. 'But I do know my mum's childhood home was in Northumbria.'

'Well, I am getting a very strong link with Newcastle,' I said. 'And I'm also getting the sense that your mother's life was quite rough and fraught and beset with a lot of problems and pain, but not physical pain.' I hesitated, reluctant to pass on some of the information I was now receiving, but compelled to do so. 'I feel that she associated with – had connections with – a lot of people who were not good for her, who she was quite damaged by. Your mother was either married more than once,' I added cautiously, 'or had many partners in her life. Would you know that to be true?'

'Yes,' Stephen replied, looking suddenly very vulnerable.

'With the greatest respect to you and your mother,' I added, continuing even more reluctantly than before, 'I am getting the feeling that your mother never really found a suitable partner and, as a result . . .' I hesitated, searching for the least painful explanation. 'She spent her life looking for that someone special who would look after her and remain with her. When, sadly, this didn't happen, she had a succession of partners. Do you know anything about this?

'Have you been looking at a black-and-white photograph of your mother recently?' I asked. 'I'm now getting the sense that something happened to your mother that was reported in the newspapers and that there is a newspaper cutting . . .'

'Yes, I've seen a picture of Hannah that was shown on television and a newspaper also published the same picture.'

'Your mother's life came to a very abrupt end,' I added. Then feeling a very unpleasant tight sensation in my throat that made me gag and feel as if someone was trying to choke me to death, I asked rather tentatively: 'Would you know if your mother had some problems with her throat? I need to know this because she's making me feel that when she passed over, it was *not* from natural causes, that someone else was responsible. I don't want to be too graphic here, but . . .'

'I'd rather you were graphic,' Stephen interrupted urgently. '*Please* tell it how it was.'

'Is that really all right for you?' I asked, meeting his eyes and seeking reassurance.

'Yes, *truly*.'

'*Right*!' I said, not looking forward to what I now had to tell him. 'Well, I feel that your mother was strangled by a man who then dumped her body in water. Please forgive me if I'm wrong,' I continued nervously. 'But I believe your mother was on the game and that she was killed by one of her clients.'

'Spot-on,' Stephen replied, his voice barely audible.

'And I am getting the feeling her murderer was a serial killer, that Hannah was one of eight victims in all. There's no known resting place for your mother,' I added, feeling very sad for Stephen. 'Or, if there is, you don't know it because your mother keeps saying: "It's a shame he hasn't got anywhere to lay flowers and that he hasn't been given the opportunity to put things to rest." '

'That's *absolutely* right,' Stephen replied, sagging in his chair. 'My *dearest* wish is to find out where Hannah has been laid to rest. I have no idea whether she was buried or cremated, but just establishing *that* will give me some kind of closure. And if there are any family members out there, I want to meet them and introduce them to my family. I want to find out what they have done with their lives and tell them what I have done with mine.'

'Your mother always felt *very* vulnerable and afraid,' I said as I drew the reading to a close.

As I had discovered throughout the reading, Stephen's case was no ordinary case, and my investigation into her death was about to take us both on a voyage of discovery as I learned more about his mother and why she had chosen to live the life that she had.

During the reading I had seen a very clear image of Hannah's spirit holding up the picture of herself that had appeared in a newspaper in the 1960s, and I now felt that *that* photograph would provide a vital clue to help me start the investigation.

When I look at a photograph of a person, it really helps me to home into their energy and how they were in life, and I decided to trawl through microfilm in the British Newspaper Library in North London to see if I could locate the picture I had seen and peer into Hannah's eyes and get a feeling about her. Maybe, in Hannah's case, as well as unlocking some of the secrets that surrounded her tragic passing, I might also be able to discover if she knew the identity of her killer.

Having arrived at the library, I set about tracking down the photo in what felt like thousands of miles of newsprint. All I knew was Hannah's name and the date that she died, but this proved sufficient to find an article that was published in the *Daily Mail* on 26 April 1964. This mentioned a 'murder trail of five "good-time" girls' and added that the police believed they had all died at the hands of a serial killer, who had been dubbed 'Jack the Stripper'.

To this day, I then discovered, the case had remained unsolved and the identity of the killer unknown.

As I sat looking at the newspaper photograph of Hannah Tailford I was aware of her innocence. I know that sounds a strange thing to say, given that she was living the life of a prostitute but, in reality, I sensed that she was very childlike and far too trusting. On the night that she passed, I also got the sense that she was feeling very vulnerable, depressed and at the end of her tether; and that, because she knew the man who eventually took her life, she had gone with him willingly. She meant no more to him, though, than any other girl. She just happened to be in the wrong place at the wrong time, and was the one he happened to pick up and kill that night.

I also got the feeling that, at some time in the past, he had been mocked and had been at the receiving end of jibes; and that he had become known to the girls as a bit of a weirdo, somebody rather strange. Sitting there in that library, I then began to sense that he had committed other acts of violence, including roughing-up a number of women, prior to the murders; and that the prostitutes were aware that he was becoming increasingly warped and was somebody they needed to be very careful around.

The article certainly backed up my feeling that there was a connection with the Newcastle area, and my hope was that if I visited the place where Hannah had spent her childhood, I would get further glimpses into her early life that would help me find the answer as to why she left home so early and why she abandoned Stephen. Once present, in her home environment, I was sure I would get a better sense of her, be able to blend with her spirit and befriend her. Having done that, I might then be shown the final moments of her life and, perhaps, learn more about the man who took her life.

When I arrived in Northumbria, I enlisted the help of John Turner, a local historian, and together we located Hannah's birthplace, a cottage that was one of several that formed a small terrace.

When we were standing outside the cottages, John said: 'The present owner of this one has invited us inside. It's a good opportunity, because, although many of the cottages have had extensive alterations, this one is in its original state.'

Once inside the cottage, although the decor had obviously been changed over the years, I felt I was stepping back in time and, in my mind's eye, I could see Hannah's mother at work at the kitchen sink.

'It strikes me that this is quite a large cottage for that time,' I said to John. 'Were they an affluent family?'

'No. I suspect they would have been lower working class,' John replied.

'I'm sensing this was a happy home and that Hannah's family were a contented hard-working family.'

'Hannah's father was a coalminer,' John explained. 'When

Hannah was born in 1934, that industry was just beginning to run down.'

'I'm aware that Hannah left home when she was only fifteen,' I said. 'And it has just crossed my mind that she might have done this because she was pregnant. Do you think that would have been sufficient reason to make her leave home in those days?'

'Oh, yes, it would have been. Although it was a major step for her to take, I'm sure the social stigma would have created sufficient pressure to force her into doing that.'

'Something I have just picked up while you were talking is the sense that when Hannah was a child she either witnessed a baby passing or was aware that a baby, connected to her parents or their friends, had died. I sense that Hannah, in her childish way, felt responsible for the baby passing over; and this helps me to understand why she never kept her own children. It was not that she didn't love them, it was because she was afraid of keeping them. She felt deeply inadequate and inferior and, in her adult life she had an overwhelming sense, because she had often been told so, that she was *incapable* of looking after children or being a good mother.' I paused, then added: 'I'm glad I came. Being here has allowed some other pieces of the jigsaw puzzle to drop into place.'

It is obvious, I found myself thinking on the journey home, that anyone in Stephen's situation, who is dumped then put up for adoption, suffers from feelings of rejection and a very real sense that they were abandoned for a reason, that perhaps they were not good enough and that their mother did not love them. In subsequent years, regardless of however loving the adoptive parents were or how seemingly normal the childhood, the loss of the birth mother would remain as something that it is difficult or almost impossible to come to terms with. The person concerned may move on and appear to get on with life, as Stephen had, but the sense of rejection and abandonment would remain as a blight on their life. In those circumstances, you can only imagine how *wonderful* it must feel to go to a psychic medium and have your long-lost birth mother come through, saying: 'You are my son. I *love* you – and I have *always* loved you. All I want to say now is that I am sorry that, because of my circumstances at that time, I couldn't cope and had to let you go. I want you to know that I am *so* sorry for having let you down.'

Towards the end of the reading I had done for Stephen, I had also become aware of another voice.

'I'm Biddy, *please* tell him I'm here, too,' the voice had declared.

When I passed this message on to Stephen his jaw had dropped and, for a moment he had been rendered speechless.

'Biddy was my mother-in-law,' he had eventually said, shocked. 'She only died a short while ago.'

So, both mother and mother-in-law, in their desire to communicate with him had linked together to come through from the other world. Love, I felt, had been very much in evidence that day and, as a result, Stephen was already a transformed character who was better able to cope with a grief that previously had dogged his life. And another joy that had come about from all that was that he could now tell his own daughter that he had been reunited with his mother – her grandmother!

During the programme, Stephen shared with the viewers the main facts of his story. His birth mother had abandoned him as a newborn baby on the steps of Exeter Town Hall. Other than that, all that he knew about his mother at the time of the reading was that she had left home at the age of fifteen, moved to London where she worked as a prostitute and had been murdered by a serial killer. It was this tragic event that had brought him to me, although I didn't hear any of this confirmed until much later. And although at the time of the reading he didn't know anything about his birth family, he later discovered that his grandmother was indeed called Annie.

Feeling I had already made a strong connection with Stephen and with Hannah I decided to join up with an expert in the Jack the Stripper case named Paul. Between us I hoped we would uncover more about the life of Hannah Tailford and the circumstances that surrounded her death. I had no idea at that moment that this part of the investigation would take me into the lair of the serial killer, and that I would come face-to-face with a malevolent spirit that would begin to stalk me.

The first venue Paul took me to was a pub in west London. 'This pub, the Shakespeare, was built in 1826,' Paul said. 'But it isn't named after William Shakespeare. It's named after a local landowner called John Shakespeare. In the 1960s, though, it was used by a number of prostitutes, including Hannah Tailford.'

Paul then led me down some creaky old stairs into the depths of the pub where there was an underground bar. Although the pub had obviously changed over the years, I felt at once that this was a place that had played a significant part in Hannah's life and that I would be able to connect with her there. It was, after all, the venue where Hannah had met many of her clients and possibly her killer.

Having stood there a moment sensing the place, I turned to Paul and said: 'What I'd like to do here, Paul, is to try some automatic writing. The way I work is very simple. I will hold a pen poised on a piece of paper and then evoke and invite the spirit people to use my hands to write a message.'

With Paul standing alongside me, I then prepared for the

automatic writing session and began to tune into the spirit world. Sure enough, it was not long before my hands began to move. The connection was strong enough but, disappointingly, the writing produced no more than a series of illegible squiggles. After several minutes, however, the energy changed and a message did come through. The sinister words '*He wants me*' appeared and the session began to take on a darker turn.

The next moment, I found myself involuntarily screwing up the piece of paper on which the words, *He wants me*, were written.

Taken aback by the suddenness of my action, Paul asked me why I'd screwed up the paper.

'I'd reached a point,' I told him, 'where I knew Hannah's spirit was moving my hands, but then the energy suddenly shifted from Hannah to a man. When he came in, I felt a sense of anger and malice that I didn't like at all and, because I felt I was about to be used by somebody I didn't want to be used by, I broke the connection by screwing up the paper. I knew that Hannah wanted to say more but, after that manifestation of anger and malice, I hadn't any energy left to remain with her.'

I was relieved, though, that, although his spirit had come through, it had come through after Hannah and he had not been allowed anywhere near her. She was completely protected in the other world.

All in all, though, it had been a very frustrating moment, a moment in which I felt my connection with Hannah had been disturbed by a malevolent force. But when I had recovered from this, it was suggested that I should go with Paul to visit another location connected with the case, this time a unit on an industrial estate. Nobody had told me anything about this place and, as I entered it, I was completely unaware of what had happened there. I learned later that it was where the killer was alleged to have taken his victims and committed the murders. In 1964 the series of brutal murders had baffled the police, who had called the killer they so hoped to catch, 'Jack the Stripper', because of the way he had left his victims bound and naked.

Not surprisingly, it proved to be a grim location which I sensed still held some dreadful memories of its past. As we entered the unit itself, a huge grey space, I experienced the first shock – a really horrible taste of blood in my mouth and I could also smell blood.

Having stood there a while, focusing on the place and the memories it held, I said to Paul: 'I am now getting a sense of a man – the killer – who used to come to where we are standing now to stow away – hide – items of clothing from his victims. There is something *really* unpleasant about this man and I am getting a strong sense that he gained sexual gratification from the terrible things that he did here.'

Pausing, I turned to Paul and asked: 'Do you know if Hannah Tailford was ever actually in this place?'

'Yes, that has been mentioned,' he replied.

I felt even more certain at that moment that the malevolent energy I had become aware of just before I screwed up the paper during the automatic writing experiment, was the energy of Hannah's killer, and that the presence I had felt then was the presence I was once again feeling.

'I'm sensing the same anger I sensed earlier,' I said to Paul. 'And I now know for sure that it was driven by sexual desire. I can feel this man's presence here and, although he can't harm me because my spirit guides are protecting me, without their presence and help, I wouldn't want to stay in this room. He is aware of everything we are doing and his eyes are watching every move we make right now.'

Feeling there was nothing more to be gained from remaining

in that dreadful place, Paul and I were very relieved to get out of there.

In the event, the visit had proved to be more helpful in unravelling the mind of the killer than bringing me any closer to Hannah, but at least I now knew what had motivated her killer.

When, to our great relief, we found ourselves outside the unit breathing in fresh air, Paul told me something really interesting. Although the unit was little more than a solid concrete box, in the 1960s there were cable areas under that floor where it would have been possible for the killer to place the bodies of his victims. I had had such a strong feeling that bodies had been buried there but although I could see that Paul was impressed by some of my findings, I was actually feeling very frustrated. Once again I had been prevented from coming any closer to Hannah by the malevolent energy of a man I was now convinced was her killer. Determined to press on, though, I decided to retrace Hannah's footsteps in the area where she used to ply her trade. This, I hoped, would provide the missing links I was looking for.

The first impression I got when I began walking those streets that Hannah had once walked was one of being very afraid. That was not really surprising. She would have been on her own as she walked and often anxious about who might walk around the corner. Like all prostitutes, she must have felt very vulnerable and fearful much of the time.

For the first time, too, she allowed me to experience the sense of loss that she had felt when she gave up her children; and, finally, as I walked those streets I became totally convinced that Hannah did know the man who killed her; that he had been in the habit of stalking her and that, although Hannah was entirely innocent of causing him any harm, he had taken revenge on her for all the jibes he had endured in the past.

The link with Hannah's killer had definitely unsettled me, but I knew the moment had come when Stephen and I should visit the place where Hannah's body had been found. This suggestion proved to be a very emotional one for Stephen and, not surprisingly after all those years of hoping for closure, the floodgates opened and he burst into tears.

We both knew, then, that it would be a roller-coaster journey back through time, but neither of us had any idea as we set out that it would turn out to be a journey that would enrich Stephen's present-day life forever.

Having followed Hannah's trail from Northumbria to the site in London where Hannah's body had lain, we discovered that she had been found in February 1964, when two brothers were on their way to the Corinthian Boat Club on the River Thames where they were going to prepare a sailing boat for a race taking place later that day. As they walked along, they noticed a woman's body and, later on, the woman was identified as Hannah Tailford. Now, forty years later, her son had journeyed with me to the site where her body was found.

'So, here we are in Hammersmith, London, by the River Thames,' I said gently. 'And this mudbank area is the place where your mum's body was found. How do you feel about being here?'

'It feels very strange,' Stephen replied, his voice choked with emotion, 'that all those years ago when I knew nothing of what was going on, my mother's body was being discovered in this bleak place. It's *so* sad. She was only thirty, but he, without a second's thought, stole her life from her. He didn't stop to think that she was somebody's daughter, somebody's mum – and she wasn't even his only victim, just one of several.' Stephen paused meeting my eyes. 'I *desperately* want closure – and this is all part of my journey towards that – but I don't feel inclined to lay any flowers here.'

Despite all my efforts, I had trouble making a connection with Hannah in that place.

'I just can't get a sense of her here,' I said to Stephen. 'And maybe that's because this is a place she doesn't want to return to. It's such a murky bleak place, I can understand that.'

For Stephen, as well as for me, it had been a somewhat frustrating journey. Having travelled all the way to London, he had come away with nothing, but he assured me that really, he felt it was better not to have had Hannah coming through in that awful place.

Still resolved to find a new piece of evidence that would give Stephen the closure he was looking for, I decided to comb through archives for the original coroner's report into Hannah's death. If I could find a clue to the whereabouts of any other members of Stephen's family, I felt I would have a chance of discovering Hannah's final resting place.

Once I had located Hannah's file, I was able to pick up on a number of useful things, including documentation of Stephen's birth and confirmation that Hannah did have four children, a fact I had picked up earlier during the initial reading; and that Stephen was the eldest of the brood. Stephen was obviously thrilled to know that somewhere out there, he had blood relatives; and we decided the next step was to find one of these in the hope that there could be a family reunion and that someone might know Hannah's final resting place.

Using information in the report, we were able to track down Stephen's cousin, Carol, who lived in the north east, and Stephen and I travelled there for the introductory meeting. Naturally, Stephen was nervous, but at another level he was *really* excited because it felt like the end of a journey that had started from a position of scepticism and ended up with joy and reconciliation.

When Carol opened the door to us, she threw her arms

around Stephen and gave him a wonderfully warm, welcoming bear-hug. Then, when we were all sitting down comfortably in her sitting-room, she said: 'I've sorted out some photographs to show you of Hannah at different stages of her life. The first is when she was about thirteen.' She then produced pictures showing Hannah as an attractive young girl teetering on the verge of womanhood and another of her with her mother, who would, of course, have been Stephen's grandmother, Annie, and another of her when she was nineteen years old.

Not surprisingly all this proved too much for Stephen and, as Carol sat alongside him, a comforting arm placed around his shoulders, he was overcome by the emotion of the moment and was consoled by Carol.

'When I first read for Stephen,' I said to Carol, 'I had a very strong sense of his mother in the room and it took a lot out of me to go into details of how she had been earning her living, and how she had died at the hands of a serial killer. It took a lot out of me because this was not the kind of stuff I usually dealt with. Normally, I like to bring people a sense of joy, wonder and reunion.'

'But it's *lovely* to have had such a good result,' Carol said. '*Lovely* for Stephen and me to meet another member of the family we didn't even know existed.'

For Stephen, then, it was the beginning of the end of a long emotional journey, but there was still one more thing he wanted to do which, until then he had been unable to do, because he had never known the whereabouts of his mother's remains.

But now that he knew that Hannah was brought home to Northumbria to be cremated, he was able to say a proper goodbye.

At last, after forty years, Stephen had got the closure he had been looking for; and I could tell he was now looking forward to the next chapter of his life, which would include meeting the rest of his extended family. I was also aware that he was no longer the sceptic he had been when he first walked into the room for his one-to-one reading, and that this change of heart had allowed him to say a much less final farewell – *goodbye for now*!

It was, beyond doubt, the happy ending that I had been hoping and praying for.

4
It's Not all Plain Sailing

I am always happy to work with the spirit world. So, when I was asked to take an evening of clairvoyance in a local church I gladly agreed. I certainly did not foresee what I was letting myself in for. By then, I had, thanks to television, had my share of fame and of being interviewed and recognised, but that did not mean I was above having humbling and humorous experiences – and there were also, I discovered, a fair number of testing moments in store for me!

One example of these – a very *testing* one! – was when I arrived at the above-mentioned church twenty minutes or so before the evening was due to commence. My welcome that night consisted of being shown into a room that was so cold my teeth began to chatter within seconds. As I stood there, my fingers and toes becoming numb, I was joined by a pleasant middle-aged woman who said: 'Can you tell me what time you would like to finish your demonstration, so I can tell the ladies in the kitchen what time to put the kettle on?'

Having glanced at my watch and noted it was coming up to seven-thirty, I replied: 'I'll be finished by about nine o'clock.'

This was greeted by a look of horror that flooded on to her face and, before I could establish what had caused this, she turned on her heels and fled.

'What the . . . ?'

There was no time for me to finish the sentence before she returned with a reinforcement in the shape of the Church President.

'I understand you want to finish at nine,' this lady said, accusingly.

'Yes . . . please,' I replied, trying to stop my teeth from chattering.

'The congregation will be v-e-r-y disappointed,' she snapped back sternly. 'I think you should work to at least ten o'clock.'

I wanted to believe she was joking, but I knew from the expression on her face that she wasn't. She clearly didn't understand that two-and-a-half hours of clairvoyance is a *very* long time, and that it is difficult for a medium to sustain the link to the spirit world for such a long duration. Our work is very draining and we cannot do the spirit-communicators justice if we exceed the natural limit. I would far rather work for an hour-and-a-half, firing on all cylinders, than three hours at a slower rate and be left with no fuel in the tank! I also think that two-plus hours are a very long time for a congregation to remain seated on hard chairs, usually in a draught, without an opportunity to ease their backs, stretch their limbs or have a toilet break.

In the event, the lady president and I reached a compromise, but neither of us was really happy with the outcome.

When the time came to leave the chilly room, I discovered the church was packed to the rafters with people standing at the back and some even perched on the edge of the refreshment tables. As I stood to give out the first spirit message of the evening, I could hear a chink-chink-chink sound emanating from an elderly lady at the back of the church who was counting out the raffle money! 'I won't say anything,' I thought. 'I'll just do my best and carry on and she'll stop soon.' I had not, however, allowed for the re-counts! Half an hour later the chink-chink of the coins was getting worse and she had now been joined by another senior lady who was helping her by ripping up the now-redundant raffle tickets.

It was like Chinese water torture, but instead of drip-drip, it was chink-chink and rip-rip. Then, just as I was relating the last precious moments of a young girl's life to her grateful but grieving mother, I was finally completely overcome by the extraneous sound-effects and lost the plot.

Pausing in mid-flow, I had to ask my tormentors to stop what they were doing. Then, feeling somewhat flustered, I attempted to regain my composure, only to be interrupted by the chairperson who, as she explained later, was 'having a senior moment' and had to leave the platform and go running down the aisle to the nearest toilet before, minutes later, clonking back on to the platform and declaring to all present, 'That's better!'

At the end of the evening, when everybody who had attended seemed happy enough, the church treasurer approached me.

'We've taken *more* money this evening than we've taken in a long time,' she said smiling and handing me a sealed envelope. 'So this is to cover your expenses for the night.'

On my arrival home, I opened the envelope and discovered that the evening had cost *me* dear! Having said that, I would like to make it clear that I am happy to give my time freely when demonstrating for a host of good causes. I do, however, need to keep a careful balance between how much unpaid and paid work I take on or I'll be dispatched, all skin and bones, to the other world before my time!

The reason, though, that I have related the above tale of comedy and woe is to convey that the work of mediums like myself is *not* all glitz and glamour. For every night of appearing at venues like the London Palladium, there are a hundred-plus appearances to be made in churches like the one above, or Red Cross halls or damp scout huts! However, as I regard the work that I do a vocation – a service to my fellow human beings – and because I am proud to be a servant of the spirit world, I regard *all* the work I am called upon to do as a blessing, and I would not wish to dedicate my life to anything other than what I am doing.

What has been confirmed for me many times over the years is that regardless of whether the connections with the spirit world are made for a television programme, or during a private reading, or on stage in front of a large audience, the spirit people always do what they can to be heard.

The conditions a medium works under, however, can make or break, help or hinder the process. We are only human and, therefore, subject to the same kind of fear of failure and trials and tribulations as everyone else. When I did a recent demonstration in Kent, for example, it proved to be quite an experience to say the least. The bar was open in this particular venue, which had some curtained cubicles around the sides for when they held evenings of erotic lap-dancing! Fast food, including chips, were also served throughout my demonstration. The DJ, who must have thought I had been booked to give some kind of 'rave' mediumistic performance, decided to warm up the audience with an array of heavy rock music. Not surprisingly, I took one look around me and decided it did not fit my idea of a suitable place to work! I knew I would be up against the so-called ambience of the place even before I started – and I was right.

The first half, which thoroughly dampened my spirits, seemed to go on forever and by the intermission I wanted to go home. When I phoned home, however, my partner persuaded me to go back out and continue the demonstration. The people, I must admit, were lovely, but the venue was entirely wrong and not in the least conducive to receiving messages from the other side. All I could do in the second half was surrender myself to the Great Spirit, and say: 'Okay, let's try to lift the energy here so that I can give as many accurate messages as possible.'

My plea must have been heard because, despite my conviction that the evening was going to be a disaster, the spirit voices started to come through thick and fast. Nevertheless, that evening confirmed that mediumship is a blend of energies and these energies can be disturbed by lots of different elements that are beyond a medium's control. It also reconfirmed that love is the most powerful force in the universe, the very essence – the marrow – of life that flows through all creation; and wherever it exists no obstacle or impediment will stand in its way. Love, as the ancient saying goes, will leapfrog any boundary and find a way.

Learning to love those we are among, whether we like them or not, certainly helps to bring about a more peaceful, harmonious atmosphere; and simply accepting that there are some things in life we can change and some things we cannot, definitely reduces the stresses and strains.

During a recent dinner date with some friends, who I have known for twenty-plus years, we were bemoaning how time flies and this encouraged us to make a pact in which we all resolved to push out our boundaries, be braver, and open ourselves up to as many new challenges and exciting opportunities as possible. Having raised our glasses to *that*, one of those present added: 'If we do this, we will be able to look back in twenty years' time and appreciate that we have made the most of our time here.' At that moment, I couldn't help remembering that someone had once said to me: 'I don't want to look back on the day I die and realise I haven't lived. A wasted life is a living death long before the clock actually strikes the hour.'

That, I thought, was *so* true!

*   *   *

As a working medium, however many new challenges I take on, I am always up for more, always open to new ways of using my psychic and mediumistic gifts. It is, I am convinced, very important for me to extend my boundaries and keep growing as a human being. No matter what our vocation is in life, I am aware that we can often fall into the trap of playing it safe and sticking to what we know. I have never been one, however, to feel the need to be in a warm cosy place underneath my own comfort blanket. I like to take the bull by the horns and travel outside my comfort zone.

In the past this attitude has brought some criticism to my door from both non-believers and those who have a more traditional approach to mediumship. Although I class myself as a Spiritualist, not all the work I undertake falls under that banner. I do not regard mediumship as something that belongs exclusively to Spiritualism, as I know the spirit world is there for everyone no matter what their religion or belief. In other words, when I work inside a Spiritualist church, I am happy to be a representative of that religion; but that does not mean I am not free to use my gifts in other arenas.

My view is that as long as I approach each opportunity I am given with respect for those I am working with, then I am happy and do not feel I am misusing my gifts. If some people regard my work on television as letting the side down, then I must accept that as their opinion. It will not, however, affect the choices I make about the work that I do. Diversity, it is said, is the spice of life and this is *why*, when another challenge came my way in the summer of 2004, I had no hesitation about accepting it. That challenge turned out to be yet another TV special, this time one entitled: *I'm Famous and Frightened 2.*

In this programme for LIVINGtv I was asked to spend three nights with eight celebrities in a haunted location to see what, if any, paranormal experiences they might have, and it proved to be a fantastic caper, one of the highlights of my year. It definitely placed me outside my comfort zone, not just because of the work that was expected of me, but because it was my first television programme away from IPM, the company that had made all my other TV programmes. This meant that I had to get used to a new camera crew, new producers, and trust them to portray my work in a way that I would feel happy with.

In truth, it is great when an opportunity like this comes along because it takes us psychic mediums outside the normal arenas in which we work and opens us up to different ways of using our sensitivities. Apart from being a huge production, with over seventeen hours of live TV, *I'm Famous and Frightened 2* also had a technical and production crew of over seventy people. I felt privileged to be involved, but also very nervous.

The programme was filmed at Fyvie Castle, Turriff, Aberdeenshire, which dates from the thirteenth century when it was used as a hunting lodge. Situated on a mound above the River Ythan, ghosts, legends and folklore galore are woven into its turreted tower history. Upon arrival, I took a few moments to familiarise myself with the location by setting off for a refreshing walk around its grounds and lochside which, I was told, had been landscaped in the early nineteenth century.

After my brief walk, I was whisked off to meet the eight celebrities who would be my castle room-mates for the duration of the show. These included Danniella Westbrook, the actress from *EastEnders*, presenter Rustie Lee, who used to be the resident cook on GMTV, and Andy Kane (Handy Andy) from *Changing Rooms*.

I realised from the first meeting that it was going to be an uphill struggle for some of the stars to open up and be receptive enough to feel the often delicate influences of the spirits as they drew close to us. Having said that, Rustie and Danniella proved to be very open and receptive; and while Handy Andy kept claiming he was 'sitting on the fence', I thought he had the ability to feel and sense not only the spirits but the residual energies that had stained the building throughout its long history. This was good because, in an old building such as the castle, it is often the residual energy that can be sensed, rather than the spirit people who still dwell there.

Rather like a stone that ripples the surface of a pond or lake, significant events, especially those which involve strong emotions like a murder or the joyous birth of a child leave an imprint of energy that can hang around for years after the people concerned have passed. All I could really hope was that the celebrities could, for the duration of time we were together, respect not only the work that I did, but also the history of the castle, including the tales of ghosts, haunted rooms and strange curses.

'I have no interest in converting you to my beliefs,' I reassured them. 'I will simply do what I do and allow you to make up your minds.'

I was, though, despite appearances, a little nervous about how the weekend would pan out and I could only trust that my spirit guides would give me a helping hand and keep me safe. Having sent out a stream of prayers to them, I knew they would not let me down, even though I was sure they would despair of me at times for doubting them.

As I made my way down to the gallery on the first night, I knew it was for a demonstration of 'table tipping', *the* event I was feeling most nervous about.

Table tipping is when we request the spirit world to make their presence known by manipulating a table. As far as I know this was the first time this particular feat had been attempted on live television, and I was aware that it might not come off. Even in a class of experienced mediums you can never guarantee results. I was determined not to back out, though, and I just decided to give it my best shot and ask my spirit guides, Zintar and Star, to back me up and do their thing!

As I joined the group for the table-tipping experiment, I could feel them watching me like a hawk and thinking: 'Table tipping, eh, where's the trick in this? Where are the wires? Where are the pulleys?'

First, though, I explained to them how table tipping works.

'You will simply need to place your fingertips very lightly on the table,' I said, smiling encouragingly at each of them.

Then, as we stood around the medium-sized wooden table, I added: 'The table will only move when the spirits join us. It is the intelligence of the spirit mind that connects with and uses the physical energy we are sending, through our fingertips, into the table.'

I also explained that I would only remain with my fingertips on the table until the moment I felt the table had built up sufficient momentum for me to step to one side and leave them to their own devices. I was not sure how this would work as, in the normal course of events, the medium remains present as a catalyst for the table-tipping phenomenon. Anyway, that's what I had decided to do – and that's what I did!

When things had built up to a real momentum, I stepped to one side and announced in a deliberately melodramatic voice: 'Okay, you are on your own now' and, to their absolute amazement, the table continued to rock, move and tilt. I am sure when I was connected to the table they thought I was pushing it, but now the expressions on their faces were an absolute picture and it was yet another occasion for me to say under my breath, 'Thank you, spirits!'

* * *

On the Monday morning, as I waited in the departure lounge of Aberdeen Airport, I found myself reflecting on the previous night's events and, as I did so, I tried to get my head around the occurrences of the last three days. Some of the strange encounters that had taken place there had really made me question my own stance on a lot of things, and none more so than that of Fyvie Castle's accursed 'weeping stone'.

The 'weeping stone' incident was certainly one of the strangest phenomena I had ever come across in my working life as a medium. Even though I know this sounds very strange, I can only say that the stone itself was like a *living, thinking* thing – an animate rather than an inanimate object – and there was a presence, and a vile pungent smell, coming from within it that grew stronger and stronger and wafted around the room when we were sitting by it trying to use our sixth sense to tap into its secrets and peel away its history.

The story behind the stone, so the legend goes, dates back to the thirteenth century when a poet named Thomas Learmont was granted the gift of prophecy by the Queen of the Fairies. During his many travels Thomas came upon Fyvie Castle when it was under construction. Included in the material used for one of the towers were three stones that had been stolen from the sacred ground of a nearby church. This had angered Thomas, now known as Thomas the Rhymer, and he had placed a curse upon the castle that meant no eldest son of the owner would ever inherit it while the three stones remained at the castle. His prophesy and curse, it seems, came true. All the eldest sons succumbed to death before they had had a chance to inherit the castle and this has remained the case until this very day.

The precise whereabouts of the first and third stone are unknown, but the first is believed to be built into the tower, and the third is believed to be at the bottom of a nearby river.

The second stone, however, the one we investigated for *I'm Famous and Frightened 2* is on display in a sizeable bowl that is needed to collect the large amount of water that still mysteriously seeps from it.

At one moment, as I stood there, looking at the weeping stone, which was a big, dusty, cobwebby-looking object, placed in a bowl with a Perspex lid, so that you couldn't touch it even if you wished, I linked into some of its history, which I truly believe started out good but somehow became corrupted along the way. I knew that there were many layers to its history, and that most of them were truly terrible. Into my mind came images of robed people conducting strange human-sacrifice rituals, and voices from hundreds of years ago chanting words that had become absorbed by the stone and were now part of its core.

Just as I thought I was about to see more, something changed, and a barrier that I could not see through came into being. This may sound freaky, but it was as if the stone itself was resisting my psychic prying and was not happy to be read. I could sense its strange power connecting with me, pushing me away and trying to enter into me. At that instant I felt Zintar, my spirit guide, draw close and I felt totally surrounded by love and protected by the spirits who work with me. Zintar did come with a warning, though. As clear as a bell, I heard him call: '*Tony, enough*' and I knew then that my time with the stone should come to an end.

All the while I was working with the stone, as horrible as it was and as vile as it felt, I nevertheless felt completely safe and protected. There really was an incredibly strong force for the good in that castle that was watching over me.

Another fascinating event that came out of that weekend at Fyvie Castle, which might even give some sceptics food for thought, occurred during an investigation I undertook with Rustie Lee in what was known as the 'Murder Room'.

Some scientific investigators, known as ParaScience, who were working with us that weekend, had placed a number of thermometers in rooms around the castle where the investigations were taking place. As Rustie and I entered the Murder Room, we were instantly drawn to one particular corner where we felt the overwhelming presence of a spirit lady. We both felt a chill down our spines and the eerie sense that we were being watched by spirits. Feeling somewhat intimidated by this we soon called the investigation to a halt.

After we left the room, the ParaScience investigators checked the reading on their equipment and discovered that the temperature in the corner of the room, where we had stood sensing spirit activity, had dropped by 3.5 degrees. Shortly after we left the room, however, the temperature returned to normal. There was no rational explanation for this.

As I have already said, some of the events that weekend caused me to change my outlook on a few things. I have never been one to dwell on the dark side, so having had to do this during the time I was asked to focus my attention on the weeping stone proved to be a real challenge for me. One thing that was confirmed for sure, however – and much stronger than ever before – was that good is always stronger than bad, light will always outshine dark and, if we ask, we will always be kept safe and protected during such moments.

I can also confirm that, however long we mediums spend in this work, there is always something new for us to learn – or have the light shone upon – and *that* is the true meaning of enlightenment!

A haunting incident that cropped up recently occurred during a visit I made to two friends, who had just started a B&B

business in an old house they had bought in Suffolk. One of the rooms in the house, which they had been told had always been called the 'music room', had started to ruffle the feathers of some of their B&B guests.

'On *four* separate occasions,' Jules informed me, 'the B&B-ers had mentioned at breakfast that they had been awakened during the night by someone playing a piano in the room and that the music by Mozart seemed to be coming from the far left-hand corner.'

'What did you say?' I asked intrigued. 'And did you tell any of them that other guests had had the *same* experience.'

'No, *absolutely* not,' Jules replied. 'We kept mum, just laughed it off, not wanting to scare any of our guests.'

'But when we investigated the history of the house further,' Fiona piped up, 'we discovered that, in the early 1900s, two pianists had shared the music room and the piano was situated in the left-hand corner!'

'So, how do you feel about living in a *haunted* house?' I asked, quite unprepared for the reply I received from Jules, who is renowned for being a no-nonsense person, who has her feet planted firmly on the ground.

'*Reassured*,' she replied. 'I've always wanted to believe that there is more to life than this one-time-around lark. And, having two ghostly musicians playing Mozart duets during the night is *very* comforting – gives me hope.'

'*That's the spirit*!' I laughed.

5
The Thin Veil of Death

Grief, as everyone who has experienced it knows, is all-consuming and every bit as painful as any physical ailment we may suffer. It seeps from every pore of our being, affecting every moment of our waking and sleeping life and, once its cold hand has touched us, we will never be quite the same again.

Due to the nature of my work, grief is something I come across almost on a day-to-day basis and, even now after all these years as a worker bringing forward messages of survival after death, I can honestly say that it is not something I have ever got used to being around. Nothing is more heart-rending than speaking to a mother or father whose lives have been destroyed by the loss of a child, or to a child who is yearning for a comforting hug from a lost parent, or a partner who has lost the soul-mate with whom they shared their life.

As we are born, it is a simple fact of life that one day we will die and, at some point, we will all lose someone we adore. Nothing, no matter what our belief or the nature of the person's passing, can *really* prepare us for such an event. Even when we lose a loved one after a prolonged illness and, therefore, have some time to prepare for the inevitable, the suffering can be just as intense. In the cold light of day there is still the harsh realisation that we have lost the physical contact and interaction; that we will never be able to hug or kiss that person again, never share a joke or a tender moment, never have the chance to say one more time, 'I love you.'

So, I don't think we can ever be truly prepared – not ever.

When my good friend Stuart's mother died from cancer in 1992 after a relatively short illness, I remember only too well how her passing affected him. After the initial diagnosis in early February, Pat went downhill very rapidly and, as is often the case with this terrible disease, the final weeks of her life were not pleasant, either for Pat or for those who loved and then lost her in March that year.

Towards the end as she started to slip into the other world, Stuart said he had prayed for her to pass and be released from the pain, but the moment the end came, he wanted her back, if only for one more minute or a second. So, even though the end was expected and desired, when it finally came the loss was just as real, just as sharp.

As I said, *nothing* can really prepare us.

Knowing that we continue past this life, past death, however, can in time alter how we continue with our own lives; and acceptance of continued survival can, over time, blunt the edges of pain; and the day will come when it is possible to think more about the times we spent with the person than the time we felt cheated when they passed. As the line in the hymn says, 'Oh *grave where is thy victory, Oh death where is thy sting?'*

Accepting that some day there will be a great reunion and, that in the meantime, we are still watched over and loved by our spirit family, goes some way to easing our grief and helping us to move on with our lives.

This, for me, is the true blessing of the work I do. When I am there, witnessing the moment someone receives proof that the person they love is still there, still very much part of their life and all its ups-and-downs, I can see the clouds that hang over them disappear and the light come back into their eyes. The transformation is often dramatic with some spirit people coming into the reading as another leaves and continuing thus until the entire spirit family has come forward to make their presence known. One effect of embracing eternity is that our whole world is turned upside down and every yardstick by which we set the rules for our life disappears, and a new way of looking at everything we do emerges. This moment, this epiphany, comes about when we realise we cannot die.

Months after the passing of Pat, Stuart was still struggling to come to terms with losing his mother, who was still young in the scheme of things. Pat was only fifty and Stuart was only twenty-one, no age at all to lose a parent. Although, at this point in his life, he had an interest in the afterlife, he had not as yet received unequivocal proof.

I remember offering to take him to the Arthur Findlay College, Stansted, which is generally regarded as the home of British Spiritualism and which had some of the finest mediums and teachers working there. Each year for its annual open day, the college opens its doors and offers workshops, demonstrations of mediumship and also one-to-one readings.

Knowing it would be packed, we arrived at the venue early and Stuart was lucky enough to book a twenty-minute consultation with an amazing medium called Jill Harland. As the day drew on and the time for the consultation came closer, I prayed that the sitting would be a success and that Stuart's mother would come through loud and clear and he would get the proof he so needed that she lived on in the next world.

On the dot, Stuart knocked on the door of the room only to be told by Jill that there had been a mix-up. The session had been double-booked and she wouldn't be able to read for him. However, not wanting to disappoint him, she added that if he was able to stay around until the end of the day she would be able to see him then. So, at the end of the day, fearing the medium would be too tired to read for him after a full day of readings, off he went to see Jill for what proved to be a really outstanding reading.

Later, as Stuart recounted details of the sitting for me, I learned that his mother had returned loud and clear and that Jill had given him accurate pieces of personal information that had included the names of his five brothers and sisters. It was obvious that this had been a life-changing moment for him. In all, Jill had spent an hour with him, three times the length of the original appointment, and it had been an hour in which Stuart's life had been transformed. It is often said that the spirits work in mysterious ways, and they certainly lived up to that saying that day. I now know beyond doubt that the meeting between Jill and Stuart was meant to be; and I can only hope that I have touched people's lives as effectively as Jill Harland touched Stuart's that day.

I often wonder how the messages I give affect people and change their outlook. I can only hope it is for the positive and that, in my own small way, I am helping people to come to terms with their grief, and maybe injecting some hope back into their lives. It is an all too often repeated criticism that we mediums 'prey on the grief of others', or that we 'take advantage of those in need', and I imagine this will always be the view of some people. I only wish they could be there to witness the impact that certain messages have; then, just for a second, they might pause in their tracks and reconsider their views or, just for a moment, make allowances for the possibility that mediums may be having a positive effect on people's lives.

Like everybody else, we mediums are only human, and getting the right measure in the work that we do is not always easy. When a person's heart is breaking with grief, it is very difficult to refuse a sitting, however drained you are feeling; I have experienced instances where loved ones, having passed to the other side very suddenly as a result of a tragic accident or violent incident, are filled with an intense need to make urgent contact with those they have left behind. It is as if they are desperate to console their heartbroken relatives and let them know that they have survived. I have also found that my mediumship works at its best when there is a real need. It is as if the spirit world responds to those who are hurting and in deep grief.

Recently, for example, in a spiritual development class that I was hosting, I noticed a very pretty young lady who had a look of deep sorrow etched on her face. Having realised that she was experiencing deep pain about somebody she had lost, I made a point of speaking to her a number of times during the course and, each time, I was aware of a great longing in her. At the end of the course, she hung back until we were the only two people left in the room. Then, plucking up courage, she approached me and said: 'Please . . . *please* could you look at this photograph and just see if anything . . .'

As the sentence trailed off, unfinished, she held out a picture of a tall broad-shouldered man in his early forties, who had a wave of dark hair brushed-back from his forehead, and deep dimples in his cheeks. In the photograph, he was holding a little girl and was smiling and looking very proud and happy. As I held the photograph in my hand and continued to look at his face, I felt a *very* strong connection, so strong that I felt as if I was merging into him. Then, almost before my brain had a chance to engage with what was happening, I heard myself saying: 'This man is your father . . . and he was sixty-one when he passed to the other world.'

'*That's right*! He was my father,' she gasped. 'And, *yes*, he was exactly sixty-one when he died.'

'He loves you *very* much,' I continued. 'And, right now, he's trying to communicate his name. It begins with H. Yes . . . I think his name is Harry.'

'*That's right*,' the young lady cried again, gripping my arm. 'Please tell him I love him, and that my mum loves him, too.'

There was actually no need for me to pass on that message because at the precise moment the young lady touched my arm there was another instant connection with him – something I find difficult to explain right up to this day. I can only say that, as I continued to look at the man's face, I felt a very powerful emotion, like an electric current or a bolt of lightning, pass through me to her. It was just as if he was giving her a loving embrace from the other world. I don't know how long we stood there with her gripping my arm. It could have been minutes, could have been seconds, but when I next looked into her eyes, she said: 'That was *extraordinary*! I *felt* my dad – I *felt* as if he was holding me, giving me a cuddle. How could it have been such a *physical* experience? How *could* it happen like that?'

'I don't know. I can't explain in words how it happened,' I replied. 'But I can confirm that it was a *very* special connection. Maybe we shouldn't ask too many questions. Maybe we should just accept that it happened and that, as the saying goes, "there are more things in heaven and earth" than we will ever understand. Let's just be happy that your dad – Harry – was able to make such a *powerful* connection.'

Later, I thought: 'Her need was *very* urgent and *very* great and somehow he knew that and he managed to reach her in the way that she needed to be reached. What could be more special than to receive a hug and a cuddle from the spirit of a loved one in the other world!'

Another instance of a spirit needing to make urgent contact occurred soon after Alison, a good friend of mine, telephoned to say that her dad had just passed away. He had been ill for two years and had finally gone home to the spirit world after an uncomfortable few months. Even though Alison had had a little time to prepare herself for the passing of her father after his prolonged illness, she was still, of course, devastated. All I wanted to do was put my arms around her and comfort her, but as I was working away from home, conducting a seminar, I had to settle for making regular telephone calls to see how she was doing.

As I neared the end of the week's seminar for developing mediums, which included a day of assessment and guidance for the talented group present, a lady student stood up and I was totally amazed when she made the following statement.

'I have a man here,' she announced, 'who has just passed. In fact, his passing was so recent his funeral hasn't even taken place yet. He has come back so soon because he wants to get an urgent message to his daughter. He wants her to know that he has made it over and is fine.'

Now, I had not spoken about Alison's bereavement or any of the conversations we had been having, but the next part of the message that came through made it clear that the communication was for me and for her.

'He is calling out the name "Alison,"' the student added, 'which I think is his daughter's name, and that's who he wants his message to go to. He wants Alison to know he is fine.'

Well, it is not often that a medium gets a message on such occasions, but I was left with no doubt whatsoever that this one was for me and Alison.

'*Well done!*' I said to the student. 'That was a really accurate message, and I will pass it on to my friend, Alison, who I know will be greatly comforted by it.'

This incident just goes to prove what I have always suspected, that there are no hard-and-fast rules as to when a spirit can return and communicate. Alison's dad had made his return just a few days after his passing; and for Alison, this was a momentous event that helped her through the early days of her grief and one that has comforted and reassured her ever since.

Colin Fry and I certainly get to visit a lot of places when we are working together on the 'Best of British Mediumship' tours and, after visiting Belfast, Limerick, Gloucester and Blackpool, we found ourselves on stage together in Manchester.

On this occasion, as we sat down to meet some of the audience after a demonstration, a slim, middle-aged lady, with shoulder-length brown hair, stepped forward accompanied by two teenage girls.

'I've been told that the messages you give are given to those with the *greatest* need,' she said, her voice breaking with emotion. 'But just how *desperate* do you have to be to receive one?'

At that precise moment, while she was speaking, I experienced an overwhelming all-encompassing grief that passed through my body and shook me to my very core. It was just like receiving a physical punch to my stomach. Simultaneously, the spirits encircled me and, from within their midst, I heard a girl's voice call out: *'That's my mum!'*

Realising I couldn't possibly do my best for the spirit-girl while there were so many people jostling around wanting to say hello and ask for autographs, I broke one of my own rules and did something I had never done before. Only too aware of the depth of the mother's pain and anguish, I gave her my private telephone number and said: 'Call me on this number and I will see what I can do.'

As she left, I couldn't help but notice that the tortured expression on her face had changed to one of hope.

Some days later, aware of just how important it was to get the message right for this lady, I went into my garden, which is my little piece of heaven and where I feel most connected to everything around me, and sat under my tree. Then I returned the lady's call.

After a few moments of tuning into her, I had a very strong impression that she had lost a child and she confirmed that this was true. Then, by my side, I sensed the spirit of a young, carefree girl – a bit of a tomboy – who was full of laughter and fun.

'*That's my mum*! *That's my mum*!' she kept saying.

Having described the child to the lady, I added: 'I have the sense that it is not very long since your daughter passed. She is coming forward again now and is telling me to send her love to you, her father and her sisters and the rest of the family. She also wants you all to know that she is well, is settling in, and she will return to you again when she has gathered the strength to do so. Above all, she wants *you* to know that you could *not* have done anything differently or anything that would have saved her. She is fine. She woke up in the other world and the spirits took care of her and explained what had happened to her.'

It turned out that the young girl had died from something that is euphemistically known as adult cot death. She had gone to bed one night and literally woken up in the spirit world.

The mother then confirmed that her daughter had only died three weeks before and that the circumstances of her death were exactly as I had described. Although I could tell that she wanted more from me that day, I also knew as we put the phone down that at least she now knew that her little girl was being well looked after in the other world. That, in itself, had eased her heart and healing had commenced.

This experience brought home to me just how desperate

some people are who attend our demonstrations and meetings. The need to receive something, 'just a few words', that will help them to know that their loved ones live on is very great indeed; and I spent a long time after that Manchester meeting pondering what happens on the other side to determine *who* comes through and *why*.

Is it really, I wondered, anything to do with someone desperately needing to receive a message or is it more to do with the ability of the spirits to make themselves known to the medium? Why would a long-dead grandfather come through rather than the daughter of desperate parents who are sitting in the audience, praying and hoping that their little girl would make herself known? And just how much say do my spirit guides have over who will be the next one to communicate? And what is it about an individual spirit that makes it possible for him or her to be seen by a medium? And is it those spirits with a plus factor – a more interesting or unusual aspect to their earthly lives – who are more able to shine through the haze that separates our two worlds?

These questions and many more filled my mind and I cannot pretend that I found all the answers. I used to think that it was those with the greatest need who received messages, but experience has taught me that this may not be the case. Perhaps it is rather more random than that – rather like winning a spirit lottery – and there is no particular order to it at all? Perhaps certain spirits connect more easily with the energy of certain mediums? Perhaps it is all part of a master plan? Or perhaps we should just be content that some spirits, if not the spirits of our loved ones, are able to connect? (Having said that I always hope that even though only eight or so people receive a personal message in any one demonstration, that the rest of the audience will be sufficiently touched by the messages to gain some comfort for themselves.)

Perhaps, too, for many of us, it is only when we are thrown into deep grief over the loss of a loved one that we somehow find the incentive, the courage to seek one-to-one help from a medium or go to a public demonstration of mediumship. Then, perhaps, to our huge shock and delight a member of our family succeeds in seeking us out. Until that moment we may have been a sceptic, a veritable Doubting Thomas, but having received a communication when we were, possibly, feeling the least worthy person present, we are absolutely *thrilled*. In my experience, nothing works better than a communication from the spirit world to help grieving hearts to heal and to bring closure in a positive way that enables us to move on without ever forgetting those we have loved.

One day, some years ago, I was doing a one-to-one reading for a lovely lady in her early forties who had light brown curly hair. During the reading I picked up that she herself was a gifted healer and I said: 'I just want to say that many spirits are coming through saying that they want to thank you for all the love that you give out and especially for the love that you are sending to the poor men who are trapped, at this very moment, in the Russian submarine disaster.'

The maritime disaster I was referring to was the huge Russian nuclear submarine, the Oscar-class Kursk, which had sunk on 12 August 2000, in the Barents Sea. This accident had occurred while the sub was on an exercise with many other ships – and hope of finding any of the 118 crew members alive was fading fast. The rescue mission, the newspapers were telling us, was in danger of turning into a recovery mission. Meanwhile, the horror of all those men having to take a breath to stay alive, while knowing that each breath was probably bringing them closer to death, was in the minds of people all over the world.

'Do you know, *that* part of your message is so spot-on!' the lady replied. 'I haven't been able to get that terrible disaster out of my mind and I have been thinking about those men constantly. I cannot bear the thought of them gasping for breath.'

'Well, one of them,' I said gently, 'a young man, a young Russian sailor, just nineteen years old, must already have passed because I can see his spirit at your side.'

'I don't know any of the sailors personally,' the lady replied, tears welling up in her eyes.

'That doesn't matter,' I answered. 'He just wants to thank you, and to say that your prayers and your love have helped him to pass to the other world peacefully and with such dignity, and that is *why* he has come all this way today to find you so that he can say *thank you so much* for your love.'

'Isn't that *wonderful*,' she replied, obviously deeply moved.

The next moment, as clear as clear could be, I heard the young man from the submarine speak his name.

'He's telling me his name,' I exclaimed. 'It's Sergei Vitchenko.'

'That's *amazing*,' she said.

And I was left with the comforting thought that she would now be able to remember him by name in her prayers and her outpourings of healing love.

A few weeks later by which time we had all heard the distressing news that all efforts to raise the submarine had failed, and all the men aboard had tragically run out of oxygen and perished, I bumped into the same lady again at a Spiritualist meeting.

'Let me speak to you. *I must speak to you*,' she said, greeting me in great excitement.

'Of course. What's the matter, darling?' I asked.

'Have you seen this? Did you see what was printed in the newspaper?' she replied.

Then, as she held the newspaper cutting aloft, I could see that it contained a list of names and thumbnail photographs of the sailors who had died in the submarine and there, in their midst, was the name and age I had received from the spirit of the young sailor when she and I had last met: nineteen-year-old *Sergei Vitchenko.*

What was so mind-blowing about this incident was *not* that I had been so accurate in getting Sergei's name, age and situation right, but the realisation that something much bigger than all of us had been at work – a miraculous universal power that had made anything possible. She had *not* known him, I had *not* known her before we met that day, and yet that young Russian sailor, Sergei Vitchenko, had been able to travel a vast distance in order to communicate through me and give his heartfelt thanks to her.

On another occasion when I stood up to demonstrate mediumship for some ladies in Liverpool, my first spirit contact came through even before I had a chance to thank people for coming along. A very determined, resolute man, he stood by my side and spoke in a low deep voice. I could see him very clearly. He had a handsome face, a muscular build and very short black hair. I was aware of his thoughts blending with mine and I began to describe him to the audience. I then went on to mention that he had not long passed and wanted to tell his family that he was now well and happy. After a few more details, a young lady stood up to accept the information I was giving out.

Now, at this point in the proceedings, it is very important for me to hear the recipient's voice because if I receive a rush of energy on hearing the person speak, this confirms that the right person has been located. On this occasion there was no doubt whatsoever that I had located the person the spirit wished to speak to.

'This is a relatively young man in his thirties,' I continued. 'And he is talking about being mixed up with a bad bunch of people and mentioning that drug-dealing was involved.'

'That's right,' the young lady said, mustering all her courage to answer. 'That's true.'

Then, before I had a chance to catch my breath, more and more details flowed through. It really was one of those occasions when I was *so* focused, *so* in tune with the spirit world, that I felt totally empowered.

'They didn't find his body until quite a while after he passed,' I said, gently. 'Then he was found in a curled-up, foetal position, lying on the floor.'

The pained expression was so obvious on the girl's face that I didn't need to wait for these details to be confirmed.

'She's my sister, my little sister,' the spirit was calling loud and clear, 'and I want her to know how much I love her.'

When I passed this on to the girl, who was obviously deeply touched, she confirmed that the man was her older brother.

Just as the communication was coming to a close, it became obvious that the young man wanted to get one last message through to his sister.

'Tell her I'm sorry and ask her to tell our mum that I am *so sorry* for all the things that went wrong in my life.'

This story illustrates that not all communications from the spirit world are solely concerned with bringing 'there is life after death' messages and survival information. Some spirits, such as the one I have just mentioned, also want to bring healing and closure to their family and friends. It really was very important for the girl's brother to try and help his loved ones to move on. It was important for me, too, yet another example of how wonderful and clear the connection can be when the two worlds are enjoined.

Human relationships can be very complex and can run the whole gamut of emotions. Alongside all the joys that loving another person brings, there can also be burdens and all kinds of unfinished business, such as grievances, grudges and a multitude of unresolved problems. If these things trouble us in life, the legacy we are left with can be even more painful when a person dies. Such pain can, in turn, hinder the closure that is needed if we are to move on and get on with what remains of our life. What could be more wonderful than being brought to the realisation that the spirit of a loved one wants to help, wants to soothe away the hurts, wants to forgive us for our foolishness and help 'restore us to our rightful mind'. To know that they live on and care enough to do this for us is like being at the receiving end of a soothing healing balm.

The following story, concerning a reading that I did for a lady called Gwen, is one reason why I feel as happy as I do in my work. When Gwen, a lady in her fifties, dressed in a floral dress, sat down facing me, she seemed very nervous and kept twisting a hankie she was holding as if trying to calm her nerves. As I started the reading, I looked her straight in the eyes and heard myself saying: 'Your mother is here and wants me to tell you that she still loves you very much.'

Before I could say another word, Gwen buried her face in the handkerchief and burst into floods of tears.

Having comforted her and given her time to compose herself, I then continued: 'Your mother tells me she was *very* ill before she died and needed a lot of care and nursing. She knows you found this very difficult to cope with and she wants you to know that she understands.'

As I finished saying this I had an almost irresistible urge to reach out and touch Gwen's face, but I managed to resist and continue with the reading. At one moment I heard the name 'Mary' being called out, and an astonished Gwen confirmed that this was her mother's name. A little further into the reading, Mary showed me a vivid image of her last moments. I saw her fall out of bed and hit her head on the floor.

'That's how they found me,' she explained, 'looking like a pile of old rags on the floor!'

When I conveyed this information to Gwen, she confirmed that this was *exactly* how her mother had been discovered.

'Please ask my mother to forgive me,' Gwen said, her voice choked with emotion.

Although I was surprised by this request, I did as asked.

Quick as lightning, Mary responded with an explanation: 'My daughter put me in an old people's home – and *that* is where I died.'

As I passed on all the details as sensitively as I could, I sensed that the handkerchief Gwen was still clutching in her hand had once belonged to her mother, and that she was holding on to it as a source of comfort.

After the reading ended, I spoke at some length to Gwen.

'My mother was *so* ill,' she sobbed. 'I really couldn't cope with her and I had to place her in a home. I came to see you today because I needed to know that she was fine in the spirit world, and that she had forgiven me.'

Thanks to Mary coming through, I was able to reassure Gwen on both counts and, as she left, I could see that a huge weight had been lifted from her shoulders. I also sensed that she could stop blaming herself for what had happened and begin to heal and live again.

'Thank you, spirits,' I said silently, as I closed the door behind her.

*   *   *

Fear is an emotion that all of us living creatures have in common, and what we humans fear most is the loss of what we have: our freedom, our possessions and, above all, our loved ones, and our own life.

The truism that there is 'nothing to fear but fear itself' is not an easy one to accept and, although I have come to believe that it *is* a true statement, I still have great sympathy for those who struggle with such an idea. I can only add that sometimes we must be patient with ourselves while we learn from hard experience.

Most of us are afraid of dying and the majority of us, however sceptical or belligerent we are in our attitudes towards mediums, would welcome some evidence that there is life after death. Understandably, given how much fear surrounds death and dying, the two questions I meet most frequently in my work are: 'Do you *really* believe there is life after death?' and 'What's it like, then, on the other side?'

To answer the first question, I always reply with a full-on, heartfelt, '*Yes* – I *do* believe there is life after death.'

Then I go on to explain that this belief is based on the personal evidence I have received throughout my working life that we do survive the grim reaper; and that so much in my experience has strengthened my initial conviction that we *cannot* die, that there is life in the spirit world, and that communication between the living and the so-called dead is possible.

I do point out, however, that, blessed as I have been with paranormal experiences, I am in a rather special position – one that has allowed me to appreciate that there is a wealth of difference between believing and knowing – and that I am fortunate indeed to *know*, beyond all doubt, that life goes on after we leave this mortal coil; that there is a spirit world and that *nothing*, not even death, can really separate us from our loved ones!

As for the second question, much has been said and written about what it is like on the 'other side'. Some say that there are great halls of learning where evolved spirits wait to help us understand the meaning of the life we have just lived and then assist us to make the transition from one world to the next. I believe, however, that there are as many versions of 'heaven' as there are people and that each of us will gravitate – arrive – in a familiar-looking place where we will feel comfortable and responsive to the 'physical' surroundings. If we are African by birth, for example, I do not believe we will find ourselves in an environment, such as Venice, that would be totally alien to any experience we had had on earth.

Whatever the individual circumstances of 'heaven' though, I believe that the predominant atmosphere of that other-worldly place is a welcoming all-embracing light, a vast harmonious space and a sense of being bathed in a love that is powerful enough to irradiate and permeate every particle of the universe.

One fear that people often express when meeting me is, 'I am not at all sure I like the idea of the dead watching over me, of them being able to see everything I'm doing.'

That's something I understand! The thought of spirits watching over us in our more intimate moments is off-putting to say the least. To be serious, though, I've always thought that C.S. Lewis put this anxiety to rest rather well. In his book, *A Grief Observed*, which was written after the death of his wife, whom he called H., he wrote:

It is often thought that the dead see us. And we assume, whether reasonably or not, that if they see us at all they see us more clearly than before. Does H. now see exactly how much froth or tinsel there was in what she called, and I call, my love? So be it. Look your hardest, dear. I wouldn't hide if I could. We didn't idealize each other. We tried to keep no secrets. You knew most of the rotten places in me already. If you now see anything worse, I can take it. So can you. Rebuke, explain, mock, forgive. For this is one of the miracles of love; it gives – to both, but perhaps especially to the woman – a power of seeing through its own enchantments and yet not being disenchanted. To see, in some measure, like God. His love and knowledge are not distinct from one another, nor from Him. We could almost say He sees because He loves, and therefore loves although He sees.

I find these lines very comforting – and I know, for sure, that our loved ones do not sit in heaven making judgements about us. If they loved us unconditionally in life, they continue to love us in this way after death; if they loved, as so many do, with some reservations, so be it. There is nothing to fear. What matters is that their love was sufficiently powerful for them to continue loving us – and wanting to remain in touch with us – after death! But it is, of course, only human to fear; and there are so many fears surrounding death – our own and our loved ones'.

C. S. Lewis, bless him, also wrote of his feeling that 'grief felt so like fear' but also very much like being an embarrassment to others. He describes seeing 'people as they approach me, trying to make up their minds whether they'll "say something about it" or not. I hate it if they do, and if they don't . . .'

Once again, that is so true of so many people's experience and, personally, I am a great believer in saying something heartfelt, even if it is only one sentence, such as: 'I'm so sorry for your loss' or 'My thoughts and prayers are with you and your family'.

Something we all need to be aware of, though, is that anger, too, as so many of us have discovered, is also part and parcel of grief. It is very difficult when we are experiencing extreme anguish to keep our patience with well-meaning people who say 'There is no such thing as death'.

'Of course, there *is* death,' the bereaved person wants to scream. 'And from where I am sitting right now, I can tell you it seems irrevocable and irreversible.'

Such reactions are totally understandable. When grief is at its peak, we find ourselves looking up at the sky, thinking along the lines of: 'Even if I were allowed to search those vast spaces, I wouldn't find the person I am looking for, see that face, hear that voice, feel that touch. Death is death – loss is loss. However many people tell me my loved one goes on, my heart and body are crying out, "*Come back, come back.*" But I know this is impossible. I know that the one thing I want most in all the world is exactly what I cannot have. Our old life together – all the significant and the insignificant things we shared – are gone and somehow I have to learn to live without you.'

Whatever it is that we believe, it is impossible to remain untouched by such anguish. When somebody dies it is natural to think of it as love cut short; a dance stopped in mid movement or a flower with its head unluckily snapped off, something truncated and therefore, lacking its due shape. When people think about the person they have lost, which in the early days of grieving is nearly all the time, they often experience the time they spent together like a film rewinding itself over and over in their heads. A film that, frame by painful frame, brings reminders of special moments and memories of when they first met, first loved, first held their first child. And comforting though these images are at times, there is still the moment when the film ends, when not being able to touch, or to hold, or hear the person's voice is overwhelming. Even if you feel, as some people do, that the loved person is still present, but in another room, it is not the same as having them alongside you, where you can see, hear and touch them, in the same room!

Even if you believe in the promise of eternal life it is still agonisingly painful to lose somebody you love, and it is all too easy for those offering comfort to make well-meaning but trite remarks and to tread on someone else's sensitivities. Finding the right moment, knowing when to speak and not to speak, is the key to comforting anybody. We need time and space to grieve and some of us need to work through a whole gamut of emotions before we are ready to accept and forgive; and sometimes when we are still feeling very disillusioned or angry with God for 'taking' our loved one, it is hard for us not to say 'Is there a God?'

The truth is that, even when you are heartbroken, you go on breathing and, however relieved you may be that your loved one's suffering is over at last, you still have your own suffering to endure. When slowly, though, equilibrium is restored, *that* is the time when a life-changing moment in which we embrace eternity can occur.

This proved to be the case after I had given a demonstration in Dublin. A few days after this event, I received a thank-you letter from a lady who had been present that night and who had been lucky enough to have received evidence of the afterlife from her father about whom she had had very mixed feelings when he was alive.

The spirit I mentioned had died as a result of self-inflicted wounds to his neck and, in the vision, I could actually see the results of his act. Having mentioned this as sensitively as I could, I also had to mention that there was a very pretty, young, blonde girl present whose life he had taken, in a moment of madness in the family kitchen, before he had taken his own life.

'He has come through,' I told his living daughter, 'to say that he is sorry. He is also pleading for your understanding and saying: "I was *not* myself during that terrible time. I'd been ill for many years, eventually diagnosed as a schizophrenic, and I really was not in my right mind at the time I killed your sister and then committed suicide."'

'I was amazed,' his daughter later wrote in a letter to me, 'because all the details you gave me were so accurate, and there was no way you could have known what a truly *terrible* tragedy had befallen our family. I was particularly moved when you said that he was now trying to *protect* us. *That* really hit home because that was *not* something he ever did when he was alive. In fact, when I was a child he abused me and always excused his behaviour by saying: "This is something you must *never* let others do to you." Because he was mentally ill, I suppose he really believed he was protecting me, but now he is in the spirit world I believe he sees how wrong he was and I think he was trying to say sorry and really wanting to protect me from harm. I have had a *very* hard time about everything that happened during those awful years, but I now feel that he has been trying to say sorry for a very long time and that now that he has succeeded in coming through to me all those hard times will start to lift. So, Tony, *thank you*. May you continue, for many years to come, bringing comfort to those who are bereaved and, in the words of Dave Allen, one of our favourite comedians who has now passed on, "May your God go with you!" When I came to see you that night, I was a broken woman, still hurting and still so angry with my father and with God, but now I feel a new person who is able to put all that grief behind me and begin anew.'

As I put this letter down and reflected on what that evening in Dublin had achieved, I thought 'Hope *really* does spring eternal.' And I can only hope that the work that I do, the messages the spirits help me to bring, and the lines that I write, will continue to bring comfort and solace to those who are grieving for themselves, as well as for others, and soothe away any hurt that may have been inflicted upon them by a loved one.

6

Blessed are the Children

In his lifetime, Kahlil Gibran, the Lebanese philosopher, artist and poet, said so many wonderful, memorable, spiritual things that I hardly know where to start – or stop! – whenever I quote him. One particular favourite of mine, however, is his answer to a young mother who, holding a tiny baby against her breast, said to him: 'Speak to us of children.' His reply was:

> Your children are not your children.
> They are the sons and daughters of Life's longing for itself.
> They come through you but not from you,
> And though they are with you yet they belong not to you.
> You may give them your love but not your thoughts,
> For they have their own thoughts.
> You may house their bodies but not their souls,
> For their souls dwell in the house of tomorrow,
> which you cannot visit, not even in your dreams.
> You may strive to be like them, but seek not to make them like you.
> For life goes not backward nor tarries with yesterday.
> You are the bows from which your children as living arrows are sent forth.

That is something I have always believed, but could never have put into words so beautifully. Children, I am convinced, are given to us as a gift from God, but we only hold their lives in the palm of our hand for a very short time. Then, like all fledglings, they fledge – fly off!

While they are still with us, though, it is our responsibility to love, nurture, guide and remind them, whenever necessary, that they are spiritual as well as physical, mental and emotional beings; and that in order to realise their full potential they need to appreciate that love is more essential to our wellbeing than any possession we may lay our hands on; that giving is every bit as important as receiving; and that the eternal is far more important than transitory things which do not last and which, sooner or later, must pass.

Our children are, in other words, chips off the divine as well as the parental block, and the most precious thing we can do for them is to help them to realise that they are so much more than flesh, blood and bones; and that spiritual progression is the most important thing to work on while they are here on earth.

Being a good parent is a tall order, and one that begins in respect for what our children are – *individuals* who have returned to earth to grow and to flourish, and to triumph over adversity, so that one day they can fulfil their life's plan and soul's journey.

I truly believe that each time we are born, we arrive complete with a mission which, hopefully, we may fulfil in that particular lifetime. Some of us may already have achieved an enlightened state of being, but have chosen for the benefit of others to return to earth as light-bearers, teachers or world leaders; others return to learn more and, hopefully, to make a steady progression towards the truth and all things spiritual. We are all, in other words, at different stages of our development, and to be a parent and play such a vital role in another soul's progression is a very special honourable mission in itself.

So, if you believe as I do, that we are born, but that the spirit world is our true home, you will not be surprised to hear that I have come across many children in my work who are particularly aware of the other world and who speak of seeing, hearing or feeling the presence of spirits in one form or another. Often when I am doing a demonstration, for example, a mother will stand up and say: 'My daughter is always seeing my dad even though he died before she was born. What do you make of that?'

'I'm not *really* surprised,' I reply, 'that children have so many experiences of the other world. After all, as they have been on earth for such a short time, their link to the other world is often so much stronger than a grown-up's. As adults we will have had a lot to contend with as we journeyed to where we are now, and some of our emotional experiences may have stunted our awareness and, in some cases, made us quite cynical and therefore sometimes puzzled or mystified by our children's reactions.'

Many mediums, like myself, begin to reveal signs of psychic ability from early childhood onwards; and, if such a child is fortunate enough to have parents who do not react negatively, but are supportive or have some understanding of such matters, all is well. It is more common, though, in our cynical western society for parents to react in a bewildered or fearful way by telling the child to stop fantasising or telling lies. In this instance it may be many years before the child's abilities return or are recognised, and much reassurance and encouragement may be necessary before that individual can make up for lost time and develop his or her gift further.

I am particularly conscious of how easy it would be for a child to be discouraged from speaking up because there were so many occasions in my own childhood when I saw or heard people from the spirit world, and I was aware that my companions were totally unaware of this. For me, to hear spirit voices was as natural as hearing the voices of my parents or friends and I never queried what was happening.

I never had a strong urge to tell my parents about these experiences. I was just happy to go with the flow. But, on one or two occasions, when I did mention such an event to my mum, she never made a big deal of it. She would simply pause in flicking her duster or putting my breakfast on the table and say: 'Oh, well, maybe it was a ghost you saw.' As she was so relaxed about it all, I was never made to feel I was strange or a freak of nature! And, as soon as I was old enough to know what *really* interested me, I read countless books on the subject and eventually found my way to clairvoyant demonstrations and discussion groups, and then joined a development circle in a medium's home where my own gift was allowed to surface and flourish.

Whether or not psychic gifts are encouraged when we are children, though, I am convinced that if the spirits want you as an intermediary, they will ensure, sooner or later, that you are in the right place at the right time, and the special gifts that you have been given will not be wasted. I have also never doubted that some children are born into this world as light-bearers – those who are concerned with spiritual matters – and, on one occasion, I was lucky enough to be alerted to the fact that one such child was soon to be born.

This event occurred a few years ago when I was doing a one-to-one reading for a lady called Alison, who was the sister of my friend, Wendy. At the time, Alison was about twenty-five years old and, during the course of the reading, I saw some spirit people draw close and stand behind her, followed by a lady who stepped forward and lowered her hands very gently on to Alison's belly. Clairaudiently, I then heard the spirit-woman announce: 'She's having a child, you know.' Then, emanating from within the area of Alison's womb, I saw a pink glow.

Without thinking, I exclaimed aloud: 'Oh! You're *pregnant* – and you are going to give birth to a beautiful baby girl.'

Alison, looking completely shocked and dumbfounded, replied: 'No *way*. I'm *not* pregnant and, what's more, I'm *not* even thinking of having a baby.'

She could not have been more adamant.

'I'm sorry I gave you such a shock,' I said. 'But I can only tell you what I see. Perhaps, although you are so sure you cannot be pregnant, you should trust me enough to have a pregnancy test. The truth is, I'm totally convinced you are going to have a little girl and that this birth will reunite you with somebody you were very close to in a previous life. The baby you are expecting was, in fact, your mother, rather than your child, in your last embodiment. When she is born,' I added, 'she will have the most beautiful blonde curly hair and she will look just like an angel.'

Apparently, I also added in a voice that did not sound at all like my own: 'By December, she will be with you – and, once she can speak, she will often refer to your past life together.'

Alison, who was a non-believer and a bit of a sceptic, received all this information in a matter-of-fact sort of way; and, although I knew I had given her food for thought on other issues concerning her life and career, I sensed, as she left me that day, that she had completely dismissed the idea that she was pregnant.

All that took place in April and, at the beginning of May, I received a telephone call from Alison.

'Guess what!' she said, sounding *very* pleased and excited.

'I *couldn't* possibly,' I fibbed.

'I'm *pregnant*,' she announced. 'And the baby's expected date of arrival is early December!'

'*Congratulations*!' I exclaimed.

'I don't know *how* you did what you did and predicted that,' she added. 'I just *can't* get my head around it.'

'Join the club!' I replied laughing. 'I'm no stranger to surprises myself.'

'If the baby turns out to be a little girl,' she said, 'I'll be even more dumbfounded.'

'And if it doesn't, *I* will be,' I replied.

Come December, the child was born.

'It's a *girl*!' I was informed. 'And we've called her Angel.' There was a pause. 'But you were wrong about one thing, Tony – she's *not* a blonde, she has thick *black* hair.'

'You can't win 'em all,' I laughed.

About two months later there was another call.

'Guess what!' Alison said.

'I couldn't possibly,' I replied, thinking this was all very *déjà vu.*

'Her hair's changed colour. She's now a curly-haired blonde who looks exactly like an angel.'

At the time of writing this book, Angel is four years old, but everybody says she is a very special little girl who seems so much older than her years. In the last couple of months she has also started to come out with the most extraordinary comments when she is speaking to her mother. A recent one, when she was trying to get her own way about what time she should go to bed, included the following: 'When *I* was your mum, and *you* were *my* little girl, I always let *you* do that!'

'What do you mean?' Alison replied, stunned.

'You know,' Angel said. 'When we were together last time.'

I have also been told that she is always speaking to the spirits when she is playing in the garden; and, in particular, she has a special spirit friend called Thomas who always seems to be around.

Poor Alison! She absolutely adores Angel, but there are times, Wendy tells me, when she doesn't know if she's coming or going; and she's not always sure how to react to some of the extraordinary things that Angel trots out.

One thing I am happy to predict, though, is that Angel is one of life's 'sensitives' who will grow up to do something really special with her life.

This entire incident was yet another confirmation that, even when the person I am reading for is giving me a totally negative response and saying, '*no – no, that can't be true*', I am absolutely right to trust the spirits and to continue to pass on what they are telling me.

I also think it is wonderful at such times to have it confirmed that we *can* find our way back to our soul group, with those we have lived with before, and that, having done so, we can play different roles in each other's life. There is something quite magical about this and it reminds me of those occasions when you are playing as a child and a playmate says: 'I know – *you* be mum and *I'll* be dad. Then, next time, *I'll* be dad and *you'll* be mum.' I used to think this was just child's play, but I now know it can be more than that – that the Great Spirit, likes to play, too!

To vary the pace of our live shows, Colin Fry and I included a segment which we called 'psychic connection'. For this we gave a psychic reading to a member of the audience. A psychic reading deals with the stuff of life so, rather than tuning into the spirit world, we focus our energy on the person's energy to reveal information about their past and present condition, and sometimes their future.

On one particular night I asked if anyone in the audience would like to volunteer for this and I duly went to a lady who was sitting in the front row of the stalls. As I studied her aura –

the subtle sphere of white or coloured light that surrounds each person's head and body – I became aware of the fact that she was very open to the other world. Then I saw a vision of her as a little child at the bottom of a garden and, in the vision, she was staring intently at something.

'You used to see *fairies*,' I exclaimed and, as she blushed to the roots of her hair, I added: 'They used to come and play with you, and you also saw them when you were having fun in the forest near your home.'

'Oh, my God,' she gasped, '*I did*! But I've never told a soul about this.'

I don't doubt that this will sound strange to some, but the wonderful thing was that, within her own aura, I could now sense the fairies, too. 'Know us, see us, we share your world' was the feeling I was getting from them as they danced around me.

'They have come back to let you know that you *did* see them and that they still visit you from time to time,' was my closing comment to her.

During my years of working as a psychic medium, I have learned not to question the spirits or the visions I receive. And, for this reason, I did not doubt the existence of the fairies or what Barbara, a friend, once told me concerning her experiences with flowers during her early childhood.

'Sometimes when I was in the garden,' she said, 'I used to stand peering down the "throats" of flowers like daffodils and tulips, and suddenly I would find myself entering them and travelling down their stems into the earth that nourished and sustained them. You would think it would be very dark and scary in there, but it *wasn't*. It was full of light, warmth, fragrance and goodness, and I was never scared.'

'Did you ever tell anybody?' I asked.

'Yes my mother,' she replied. 'And when my brother,

Henry, overheard me, he said: "She's being naughty, Mummy. She's telling lies." "No, she isn't," my mother said, looking deep into my eyes. "She has a special gift. She's telling the truth." '

'And can you still visit the interior world of the flowers?' I asked.

'No,' she said sadly. 'I grew up – and began to doubt myself. But I've *never* ever forgotten what it felt like to enter them and stay a while.'

Since beginning my work as a psychic medium, I have discovered that many children have special gifts which, for a variety of reasons, can be lost along the way. Many, for example, have what grown-ups call imaginary friends. But are they, I ask myself, *really* speaking to imaginary friends or to spirit friends or even their guardian angel? Some of these so-called imaginary relationships last for years and many children insist that the chair next to them at the table must be left empty for their friend to occupy. Some of these imaginary beings are given names, some are simply referred to as 'my friend'. It is a well-known phenomenon in childcare circles and one that is always accepted or dismissed with a benign smile and the words: 'Don't worry – he/she will grow out of it.' Sadly, many do and a wealth of 'other worldliness' is missed out upon!

So, here's my special plea. Pause before dismissing fairies or other elemental nature spirits or imaginary friends. Give them the benefit of the doubt and accept that there may be more residents in this world than we have yet realised.

Personally, I have always believed in what are described as Nature's elemental spirits – beings that inhabit forests, woodlands, marshes and reedbanks – and, once when I was a child and walking through a wood on my own, I was fortunate enough to catch a glimpse of one of these. Standing about two feet tall, this spirit looked like a little old man who had been camouflaged in all the colours of the woods; and, when he saw me, he paused just long enough for me to see him before he vanished. If he hadn't paused, I would have thought my eyes were playing tricks and deceiving me but, as it was, I had time to appreciate that he *really* did exist.

Recently, when I related this incident to Jill, a very rational clairvoyant who has her feet planted firmly on the ground, she said: 'Well, I must confess that up until a few years ago, although I believed in this world and the next, I gave no credence whatsoever to elemental spirits. Then something occurred that made me think again. One day when I was at home cleaning the windows, I saw something so surprising that it stopped me in my tracks and quite took my breath away. The garden, at the back of our house, had a stream running through it and, as I looked up from cleaning the windows, I saw what I thought at first was a sudden gush, a spiral of water rising up out of the stream. But, as I stopped doing what I was doing and stood there, I saw to my astonishment what I can only describe as a perfectly formed miniature person, who I now know was an orange-and-green-coloured water sprite. It hovered and danced there for a moment or two, then realising that it had been seen, it shook the droplets of water off its tiny back, plopped back into the water and disappeared from view. "Good heavens!" I exclaimed as I ran across the lawn and stood peering down into the water where it had just been. Although I didn't see it again, I was *so* delighted to have been proved wrong about elemental spirits that I walked about in a daze for the rest of the week.'

I was so pleased that, like me, Jill had received personal confirmation that elemental spirits did exist.

When you are a child and your gran tells you, 'There are fairies living at the bottom of your garden,' you don't question it, just take it for granted and think: 'Of course there are.' I never actually saw any at the bottom of our garden, but I always believed without question that there was something magical living there among the flowers and the shrubs, and I am never surprised when I meet people who have seen them and talked to them. Recently, for example, when I was doing a reading for a grandmother, I told her that she would be moving quite soon to a four-bedroomed house that would be surrounded by fields where fairies had been known to play; and that there would be an ornamental watering can in the garden that would prove to be of some significance.

Some months later she did move into a four-bedroomed house, surrounded by fields and, lo and behold, there was an ornamental watering can in the garden! She also had to admit that it was exactly the nooks-and-crannies kind of garden that she had seen illustrated in books about fairies. A very down-to-earth person, she was even more surprised when her grand-child, a little girl, kept coming in from the garden, where she loved to play in the area by the watering can, relating stories about what she had seen and the little people she had been talking to and playing with.

When I was told this, I said: 'Well, that's a variation on a theme. It's usually grannies who tell their grandchildren about fairies at the bottom of the garden not *vice versa*! To be serious, though,' I added, 'I must confess that I believe that everything in creation, whether it is a person or a pebble, a woman or a flower, or a man or a tree, has an element of their Creator, within them. And that there are also times when elemental creatures that are closely connected to the elements of earth, fire, air, water and ether, choose to show themselves to us in the form of a fairy or a little man or a water sprite.'

Time and time again in the work that I do, I find myself returning to that old saying: 'There are more things in heaven and earth' than we will ever be able to explain; and, time and time again, I am aware that the closer we come to nature and its awe-inspiring majesty, wonder, beauty and mysteries, the closer we come to our Creator. Many are the times when I feel like bounding up to people and asking them to pause a moment to look into the face of a sunflower, or observe the blood-orange glow of a sun setting, or sense that magical hour between dawn and daylight – or dusk and nightfall – when, just for a few moments, the whole of creation seems to hold its breath and is permeated with the most extraordinary stillness and silence.

'Do you *see* what I *see*?' I long to say. 'Can you *feel* the presence of our Creator? This is one of those awesome moments when the Great Spirit is inviting us to stay awhile and reflect. "Just look, listen, watch," he seems to say, "and you will realise that *that* which created you is here, there, *everywhere*."'

Stepping into this wondrous presence, then, is not so very difficult. Indeed, we could say that, at the very least, we are given two special opportunities a day – one at dawn, one at dusk – and that, in between, there are a few extra times on offer that could be listed under the heading: '*Seek and ye shall find*!'

The first time I dared to hug a tree, for example, I felt a little self-conscious and rather foolish, but once I got past those two limitations I was astonished by how rewarding the experience proved to be. Trees are *so* rooted, *so* sturdy, *so* strong and, unlike us, they lead a dual existence experiencing life *above* and *below* the earth; and they enjoy the kind of lifespan that we can only dream of.

When I stand hugging a tree that has existed for hundreds of years, I am always aware of the stability and sense of balance that exists within it and I am very conscious that, over the years, while so many of us have come and gone, it has remained standing there, a tower of strength and a silent witness to so many historical events that have taken place in that particular location. And, on the occasions when I have allowed the energy within it to blend with my energy, I have been left with a sense of renewal, of greater stability, of having *my* feet planted firmly on the earth, and I have always left its side feeling less fragmented and much more whole. It is as if certain elements within me have absorbed some of the special qualities of the tree and allowed me, at a subtle level, to get things into perspective and to become more stable, more spiritually balanced.

Having had such experiences, I am saddened when I go into cities to see so many young people who have lost contact with nature and who are living in a concrete jungle seemingly unaware and untouched by the wonders this earth has to offer. It is as if, through no fault of their own, their senses have been blunted, deadened, almost to the point of extinction, by all the mayhem that exists around them, and I long for them to be given the opportunity to escape and experience joy in the simplest of things. These concrete jungles that we are so fond of creating, devoid of parks, streams or quiet spaces, with their incessant assaults on our senses, can't but help to take a toll on the human spirit.

I find it interesting that as life becomes more and more removed from all things spiritual, people react in two ways. Some people, who have had enough of the trials and tribulations involved in living from one unnatural 'fix' to the next, do not want to believe that there is more to come and there is life after death! Others, having touched bottom, are filled with the longing to be given a second chance and rise again.

Please let somebody be there for them when they're ready to reach out, is my prayer. And, in my heart of hearts, I know there will be.

There is, I have discovered, no grief that can be compared with what a parent experiences when they lose a child. *Everything* in a mother and father is geared up to wanting to protect their child from harm – including illness and accidents. Not surprisingly then, when a child dies they are left distraught and often burdened by the thought that they have failed in some way, that they should have been able to play King Canute and turn back the tide before death took their little one from them. 'If only I'd been there . . . If only . . .' Such anguish goes to the very depths of their soul and rises and spills over time and time again. In the depths of despair, some turn upon God, shake their fists and say: 'What *manner* of God are you to allow this suffering, this accident, this mishap to happen to an innocent child?'

Anger is a natural part of loss and it must be allowed to take its course. When a person is sobbing his or her heart out, or shaking the proverbial fist at God, this is *not* the moment they want to be reasoned with or offered wise words. This is the moment when they need to feel comforting arms around them, and loving words to help them through the day, the night, the terrible void that has been left in their lives.

There are so many things in life and death that cannot be satisfied with glib answers or pontifications about what the divine purpose may be for that particular individual, and the death of a dearly loved and heartachingly missed child certainly fits into this category.

What I do know, though, from my experience of the spirit world, is that, however brief the baby's or the child's life, a very special welcome awaits those who depart this earth at such an early age. They may be here for just a short time, but they touch our hearts, call upon reserves of love and nurture that we had no idea existed within us, and they leave us all the richer for their presence. The expression 'short but sweet' was never more apt than when applied to a child's brief life; and when the agony of loss and anger and bewilderment starts to subside, we will be left with a sense of thanks that our lives were intertwined during that time we spent together; and we may even be able to accept that one day, not so very far away from now, we will meet again. Meanwhile, to comfort us, we can only pray that all that is good, true and beautiful in this world and the universe will come to our aid, soothe our suffering and help lighten the load we are currently bearing.

Will we meet again? *YES*. How can I be so sure? The spirits, including those of children, have told me so – and begged me to let others know. Many also come through with messages for their loved ones. This is not, however, something that can be hurried.

Once, for example, when I was doing a demonstration in a church in Vauxhall, London, I was approached by a young lady who had succeeded in sneaking past my chaperone during the interval.

'*Please*,' she implored. 'Can you help my friend? She's in such dire need of a message.'

'The messages,' I explained as gently as I could, 'go where the spirits direct. They have little to do with me.'

I could see that she was very deflated by this answer, but I felt there was nothing else I could say other than to wish her and her friend well.

The spirits, however, must have been listening to this exchange, as became evident during the second half when I started giving the last message of the evening. Having given out the description of a boy, aged about fourteen, who was looking for his mum, I saw, to my surprise, that it was the young lady's friend whose hand shot up.

'Do you recognise this child?' I asked.

'Yes–*yes*,' she replied, weeping.

'He is telling me he died in water when he was messing about with his two friends.'

'*Yes*.'

'His body was found in a water grid?'

'Yes – oh, *yes*.'

'He's telling me he is here because he loves you *very* much and wishes you – and a young lady he also had a great love for – to know that he is now safe.'

I waited a moment until the mother was sufficiently composed to go on listening, then I added: 'He is now talking about the month of August and has mentioned the fourteenth as the day he passed on.'

'That was the day he died,' the mother cried out. 'Oh, my God, it *is* him – it *really* is him.'

It is moments like this that make my work so worthwhile, and it is contacts such as this, which include vital evidence that a person needs, that give me the encouragement I need to keep on working on behalf of the spirits.

After attending one of my demonstrations, Jemma, a journalist friend, said to me, 'What's really cool about your readings, Tony, is just how accurate you are in the information you give.' She was most excited about a connection I had made for a lady called Tracey. I had gone to her and described the spirit of a boy of around three or four. Tracey confirmed the description fitted a friend's son who had died aged three and a half.

'His death was a big shock, *very* sudden,' I told her. 'And there was something odd about the last couple of days of his life. He was in this world one moment and in the spirit world the next.'

It turned out that the little boy, named Stephen, had been

badly burned in a house fire. His mum was at his hospital bedside when he opened his eyes and said: 'I love you,' then closed them again. A short while later, he died. On the night of the demonstration, my description of the suddenness of the boy's death was readily accepted as correct.

'He looked on you as his mum,' I added. Later I learned that at the time Stephen died Tracey didn't have any children of her own. Her friend had Stephen and a young baby, so Tracey often helped out and because of this he called her his 'second mum'.

A bit later still, I added: 'He's indicating a little girl who is alive. It's his sister. He's showing me that she has a scar on her forehead. He's touching it with his finger.'

His sister, it turned out, was also badly burned in the same house fire, and her face was badly scarred. Tracey thought that this was *why* Stephen had pointed to that part of his sister's injuries.

'He was wearing blue pyjamas on his last night,' I continued, and Tracey confirmed that this was indeed correct.

'Now I can see him taking the cord out of his dressing-gown and whipping people,' I said, amused. Tracey told the audience that he was always removing his dressing-gown cord and would playfully whip whoever would let him.

'He's telling me you bought him a pair of slippers with ladybirds on them.'

'Yes, that's right,' Tracey gasped. 'And a pair of boots, too.'

'Now this *is* very strange,' I added. 'He's showing me him putting his fingers into your mouth and you biting them?'

'He hated having his fingernails cut,' Tracey explained. 'But he would put his fingers into my mouth and let me chew the nails shorter. He wouldn't let anybody else do it.'

'By the time you were told of his condition, he had already passed,' I added.

'That's so true! I was out of the country when Stephen and his sister were so badly burned.'

'I'm getting the times two-thirty and also four-ten,' I added. 'I don't know if it was two-thirty when he was taken ill and four-ten or four-thirty when he . . .'

'Two-thirty was when Stephen died,' Tracey interrupted. 'And four-ten was when my son was born, but not on the same day.'

As reported by Roy Stemman in his book, *Spirit Communication*, later Tracey was quoted as saying: 'I realise that my experience of spirit communication, however stunning its accuracy, will not convince all the sceptics. Each person has to go to a medium and make up his or her own mind. I only know that Tony told me things that no one in the world could have known. I've received a number of messages from mediums in the past, but I still can't believe some of the things that he came out with. In fact, I couldn't sleep that night. I kept turning it over in my mind. It was *amazing*.'

I was delighted for Tracey – and pleased for everybody else present in the auditorium that night. Thanks to Stephen coming through, it was a momentous evening that provided all of us with a renewed affirmation – or a first-time confirmation – that there is life after death. Above all, I would like to think that those of us who are blessed with this 'knowing' and 'understanding' can go on to become better human beings. Getting a message from a medium can certainly have a knock-on effect on our life and our life's journey.

One day, when the sands of time have run out for us in this lifetime, we will all know whether or not there is life beyond death. But knowing this in advance can help us, I believe, to use the allotted time on this earth to shed all the unhelpful embellishments and limitations that stand between us and the truth about ourselves: that we are spiritual as well as physical beings, and that within us is a divine as well as human spark that can enable us to prepare for the afterlife and the lives to come.

In other words, the sooner we expand our spiritual horizons to acknowledge the divine spark within – and embrace eternity – and live our lives accordingly, the better.

As believers – or witnesses of paranormal events – we are truly blessed and have a chance to let our spirit, and the spirits of our loved ones, shine through for the benefit of ourselves and everybody else whose lives we touch.

Shortly before the end of a demonstration in Bristol when Colin Fry and I were running out of our allotted time and had reached the point in the evening when we shouldn't try to make any more links, I became aware of the spirit of a little girl-child wanting to make contact with her mother. Compelled to speak, I said: 'I'm receiving information that somebody who is sitting about five rows back in the auditorium has lost a child. There isn't enough time left for me to go into this right now but, if you think this could be you, please feel free to come and speak to me after the show when Colin and I are meeting people in the foyer.'

I ought to know better by now! When we arrived at the front of the theatre, there were about four hundred people waiting to say hello. In due course, however, one of the organisers brought forward a lady named Donna.

'Darling,' I said. 'Is it you who has lost a little girl-child?'

'Oh, *no*,' she replied, looking completely crushed. 'I lost a little boy. I was *so* sure the message was for me, but it *can't* be.'

'I'm *so* sorry,' I replied. 'But the spirit I referred to earlier was definitely a little girl.'

As Donna made to walk away, she looked *so* devastated I just had to call her back.

'Wait a moment,' I said, looking deep into her eyes. 'Let me see what I can do.'

Almost before I had time to finish the sentence, a little boy-spirit came flying through.

'I now have a little boy here, who's aged about two,' I said to Donna.

'*That's right – oh, that's right,*' she murmured.

'Oh, darling,' I added. 'He's showing me that, just before he passed, he had lots of tubes attached to his body.'

'Yes,' she sobbed. 'He did.'

A second later I experienced a horrible feeling of muzziness in my head and, when I mentioned this to Donna, she said, through her tears: 'They drilled a hole in his poor little head.'

'But he's saying he's feeling absolutely fine now and that he's ten years old,' I added.

'Oh, dear God, *that's right*!' she gasped. 'If he'd survived, he would be exactly *ten* now.'

'He's repeating he's fine now and saying that he wants you to feel happy, rather than sad, when his birthday comes round each year. He's aware that you have kept all his things and he likes it when you sit holding his little vests and shirts. He's also saying that however many years you may be separated, you will always be his mum and he will always be your son.'

It was *so* lovely in those difficult circumstances, amidst all the hustle-and-bustle of the queue of people wanting to come forward and say hello or get their programmes signed, to be able to pass on such a simple and loving message to ease Donna's bruised and battered heart.

'I've tried *so* hard to reach him,' she murmured, through her tears. 'And been to *so* many mediums, but this is the first time I have heard what I have always longed to hear: that he is okay now, no longer suffering, and that we will be reunited one day.'

Something else I gleaned that night was: however uncon-
ducive the surroundings may be, if we are willing to look deep
into the eyes of somebody who is in dire need and crushed by
grief, the spirits *will* respond, *will* come forward. I was so glad
I was moved to call Donna back when she began to make way
for other people in the queue. If the contact had not been made
that night, she would have remained a brave lady who, for the
benefit of others, would have continued her struggle to smile
on the outside while crying on the inside. Now, however, she
had a degree of closure and could start to look to the future
with a sense of hope.

One day I found myself reading for an English woman called
Val who, many years before, had emigrated to Australia. Now
back in the UK on holiday, she had been encouraged to consult
me by a couple of her relatives who had been to see me on a
previous occasion. I could tell, though, as soon as she entered
the room that she was *very* uneasy about the visit and had only
come to please her family who had thought it would be a
memorable holiday treat.

'I'm a staunch member of the Salvation Army,' she con-
fessed when I was helping her to relax. 'And I can just imagine
what my friends would think if they ever found out I had
consulted a psychic. But then, I've always prided myself on
being an "in for a penny, in for a pound" sort of person and I
don't want to disappoint my relatives.'

About halfway through the reading when she was obviously
impressed by some of the factually correct information she had
been given, I felt the spirit of a little girl come forward and
stand behind me. Although I knew instinctively that this child
was not directly related to Val, having questioned the spirit
further I knew I should tell Val what she was telling me.

'I have the spirit of a young girl here,' I said to Val. 'And she has just told me that she is the daughter of somebody you know very well. She wants you to give a message to her mother, who still keeps a lock of her blonde curly hair in a silver locket she wears around her neck.'

'I *can't* think what that's about,' Val replied. 'None of my friends has lost a child and I've never seen one of them wearing a silver locket.'

'Oh, well, just keep an open mind and see what happens,' I said.

Some weeks later, I heard from one of Val's UK cousins that the mystery had been resolved.

When Val returned to Australia, she had eventually found herself confessing to some friends at a Salvation Army party that she had been to see a psychic while on holiday in the UK.

'Before you all go off at me,' she added, 'I'd like to say he told me some *really* accurate things and was *really* good.'

Far from being judgemental, her friends, having got over their initial fit of the giggles, had egged her on to tell them more.

'The only thing I didn't really get,' Val added, 'was when Tony, the psychic, mentioned somebody very close to me who had lost a child and then said that the mother still wore a lock of the little girl's hair in a locket around her . . .'

Hearing a sharp gasp, followed immediately by a sob, Val was stopped in her tracks.

'What's the matter?' she asked, placing her arms around her best friend's shoulders.

'I've *never* told anybody this,' her friend replied, struggling to compose herself. 'But many years ago, when I was only a snip of a girl, I lost a baby.' Then, bursting into tears again, she pulled forth a silver locket she was wearing around her neck. 'To this day,' she added, 'I still keep a tiny lock of her hair in this.'

Val was then able to comfort her friend by giving her the rest of the message she had been given: 'Your long-lost daughter asked me to tell you such a *lovely* thing,' she added. 'She said, "When you find my mother, tell her I love her and that I want to thank her for keeping the lock of my hair in her locket. Please tell her, too, that I am *so* looking forward to being reunited with her one day."'

What I find wonderful – and *interesting* – about this particular event is that, although it defies logic that spirits should come through to people who, seemingly, haven't a clue as to why such messages are being given to them, the spirits know what they are doing; they are determined, despite all the recipients' protestations, that I should pass such messages on. That little spirit-girl, for example, doubtless knew that her own mother would never go anywhere near a psychic medium for a reading, and she took what would probably be her one-and-only opportunity to come through to Val, her mother's friend, while she was in the UK, and give her a message for her mother back in Australia.

These kind of incidents also clear the air for those people who are always saying: 'Yes, we agree that mediumship is a wonderful thing, but is it not telepathy, an ability to read people's minds, rather than being in contact with spirits in the other world?'

The answer is: 'No, it is *not* telepathy – or just a matter of reading somebody's mind – and this is proved in instances, like the one above, where the medium gives messages to people who have no knowledge whatsoever of what is being said. If they haven't a clue, how can we possibly read their minds!' The medium's role is to trust the spirits and pass on their messages even when the message does not seem to make any sense and may be greeted with complete disbelief, denial or even hostility.

*　　*　　*

On average, I visit Gibraltar about three times a year. I love working there because, although I can't quite put my finger on it, Gib is a place where spirit voices come through as clear as a bell and where I have, therefore, given some of my most evidential messages. I really don't know why this should be, but when I am working there it's just like having a telephone link to the other world. The trip I am about to recount was no exception.

Towards the end of an evening demonstration, I became very aware of the spirit of a young lad standing at my side. Having invited him to come closer I began to blend my mind with his so that I could interpret his thoughts more clearly.

'I was sixteen when I died,' he told me and he showed me a vision of himself lying face-down surrounded by water.

After I had related what I had seen and heard to the audience, a young fair-haired lady at the back of the hall raised her hand.

'My brother was just sixteen when he died,' she told me. 'And his body was found in the way you described.'

Soon the messages from the young man began to flow through thick and fast, and the young lady kept nodding and confirming all the intimate details and associated memories about the times that he and she had spent together. Then, all of a sudden, the mood changed and I heard him say in a very firm voice: 'I was murdered.'

Now, I am sure you will not be surprised to hear that this kind of information is very difficult to pass on, especially when it comes through in an open meeting in a public place. But, over the years, I have learned to trust the spirits – and my guides – and to pass on, as delicately as possible, the difficult messages I receive. When I did so on this occasion, the young lady lowered her eyes, wiped away the tears running down her cheeks, and cried out: 'Oh, my God, that's *true*! He was murdered.'

I then had a vision of the boy's last moments flash before my eyes and, once more, I told her what I had seen. It was not easy. What I had seen was very unpleasant and I had to detach myself from the vision, so that it was rather like watching something unnerving and shocking, but unreal on TV. The boy had been menaced and then attacked by two men. It was a particularly barbaric and vicious assault, but I only gave his sister the minimum of details in order not to compound or add to her grief.

Once the heartache of all this information had settled down, the young boy passed on some wonderfully reassuring messages for his sister to pass on to his mum, and then he pleaded with the family not to avenge his murder.

There is a postscript to this story. A few days later when I was enjoying a brief walk in the sunshine down Gibraltar's Main Street, a middle-aged lady caught my eye. As her face lit up and she gave me a beautiful smile, the young man's voice came once again into my mind. This was a surprise because such things do not usually happen when I am not working or consciously opening up to the spirit world.

'That's my mum,' the voice said.

With that, the lady approached me and I noticed that she was clutching a small crucifix that she was wearing around her neck.

'Thank you for the messages you gave us the other night,' she said. 'And *please* tell my boy that I love him.'

Without saying another word, she smiled, turned on her heel and walked swiftly away.

I knew her son knew that his mother still loved him and I believe she knew that, too, but sometimes it helps to give voice to our emotions. The physical separation that comes about when someone we love is transported to the spirit world is not the end of the love-bond that we shared in life. We continue to love them and they continue to love us just as much – just as intensely – as in life.

That mother, despite her grief and deep anguish about the manner of his passing, still loved her son with every fibre of her being, and I felt blessed to have played my small part in their love. This is why, however often I am away from home – and however hectic my life is – I would not change it for all the tea in China! Seeing the peace etched on that woman's face – a peace that had come about from knowing that her child lives on – was absolutely priceless. I would not have missed it for the world!

7
Our Soul's Purpose

The old saying that one person goes into a garden and sees nothing but flowers while another sees nothing but weeds is, I have found, so very true! Perhaps the latter situation comes about because so many of us are *so* wrapped up in everyday concerns that there is no room for anything new to enter. We can, however, change this state of affairs, and for starters all it takes is the simple realisation that we will never see beyond the cares of this world unless we learn how to shift our focus – mentally, emotionally and spiritually.

What we need to do, whenever we can, is to work at creating a space in our mind, so that we can be open to the bigger picture – to the life that exists alongside and outside our personal situation.

Creating a space, then, can have a *really* positive influence on our day-to-day life, and one that will ultimately help us to realise that we are never ever truly alone. Opening ourselves up to creation – and to the influences of the next world and all those who dwell there – while remaining in touch with our own soul, can give us a sense of comfort and the will to overcome any obstacles in our path. Appreciating we have a soul is just like discovering that we have a best friend or spiritual advisor dwelling within us – somebody who is there for us twenty-four/seven.

The truth, as I see it, is that we are surrounded by love and support that is just a prayer or a thought away, and it is always there for us to tap into. And all that is needed to truly appreciate this is for us to learn how to heighten our awareness and tune into the positive elements of our lives. Then all the doom-and-gloom will take on a new perspective and will no longer have the same power to swamp us and draw us into a place that stifles our spirit.

One simple way we can heighten our awareness is to make use of our five glorious senses – hearing, sight, taste, touch and smell – to help us to come into the present, be where we are, and leave behind all the usual mind-numbing day-to-day worries and preoccupations.

Let's begin by imagining we are sitting together in a large, light, spacious room; then look around and appreciate the light, colour and texture of each animate and inanimate object. There is no need for us to comment mentally on what we see, we just need to look, let things be and become aware of the life within each thing.

Next, let's listen to the nearest sound(s), then let our listening run out to the furthest sound(s). We need not comment on what we hear mentally. Just listen and become aware that each sound arises out of silence – out of the ether – and that there has to be space and silence in order for individual sounds to be heard.

Let's touch something – a tree, petal, stone, brick, pencil, piece of material, *anything* – and feel its being, the life within it. A wooden pencil, for example, was once part of a tree that was nourished by earth, air, sun and water.

Let's taste something – a sip of refreshing water, a sweet or piece of fruit and *really* savour it.

Now let's close our eyes and smell something – a rose petal, a leaf from a herb, our favourite soap, fresh bread – and delight our nostrils.

Let's become aware of the rhythm of our breathing, experiencing each breath flowing in and out, and enjoying the life-giving force and air circulating around our body. Just allow everything else to be, both within and without.

By the time we have completed these simple exercises on the reawakening of our five senses and heightening our awareness, we will have moved out of our usual preoccupations with the past or the future and will be experiencing the present moment.

Having arrived in the present, this is the moment for us to go into the garden, if we are lucky enough to have one – or stand by a window if we have not – and just sense the transformation that comes about when we allow ourselves to be lifted, set free, however momentarily, from all the usual burdens that render negative all that could be positive in our lives.

There is, as they say, no time like the present, so let's pause now and ask ourself: When was the last time I listened, *truly listened*, to external sounds – sounds that silence my inner circling thoughts and nourish the mind and bring me to a sense of inner peace? Wherever we live – town, city, hamlet or village – there is always something of beauty to listen to. There is the song of the blackbird at dawn or twilight; the sound of pigeons or doves cooing; the sound of the wind or rain; the sound of children laughing.

To become aware of such things, though, we need to withdraw our focus, however briefly, from concerns with the past or future and come into the present. When we do this, we will sense something we had temporarily forgotten: that there is order in the seeming disorder and chaos of everyday life; and there is that eternal presence, that '*peace that passeth all understanding*' residing within us.

Another bonus that comes about from truly learning to listen and heightening our awareness is that we also become better listeners when it comes to our relationships with others, and that can have a very life-enhancing effect for them and for us!

Embracing that which is eternal, then, through learning to focus our attention on each of the five senses – hearing, sight, taste, touch and smell – is within our means, and it will increase our sensitivity and have a positive effect on our lives whenever we take a few minutes to tap into it.

I am not suggesting that all our problems will dissolve, as if by magic, while we are doing the above exercises and taking a pause from the usual run-of-the-mill thoughts and everyday concerns. I am simply saying that most of us have over-burdened over-cluttered minds that are crying out for periods of rest and relaxation from everyday matters; and that we can nourish our entire being simply by coming into the present and letting things *be*.

Those two time-honoured sayings, 'let it be', or 'let things be' are incredibly wise.

Most of us find it very difficult to believe that it is possible to free ourselves of negative thoughts and emotions. Yet so many of our problems are kept running by the sentences we repeat in our heads. As vulnerable human beings, our attention is always becoming attached to something or somebody, and it commonly becomes attached to our own particular set of problems. This is why, for so many of us, a large part of our sense of self becomes bound up with our everyday problems and we lose sight of what is truly important.

Some of us even get angry when it is suggested that we can free ourselves of negativity if we wish. This is not surprising! Having invested so much of our time and energy in troublesome thoughts and feelings, our sense of self – our identity and the person we think we are – often becomes totally entangled, albeit unconsciously, in this state of affairs. And when this happens it is so easy to lose sight of all the wonderful things and the lovely people around us. Sometimes, too, it is as if we fear being without our problems. What would be left if they were suddenly dissolved, given up, stripped away?

Perhaps it is only when we are *truly* fed up with feeling down, *truly* had enough of negativity, of the bad taste that it leaves in our mouth, that we can decide that we are not going to put ourselves through these particular hoops any more, that we want to live a different kind of life – a *positive* life.

At such times it always helps to remind ourselves that good can come out of the worst situations – and that the happy-ever-after ending, which is so fondly portrayed in fairytales, is a possibility. Yes, life can be hard, can test us to the limits, and it's no wonder that sometimes we find it hard to cope, but these trying times can have a positive side. They are an opportunity for our soul to learn and to make progress, and to shine through adversity. It is *how* we cope with such challenges that makes us the people we are.

Sticky patches, then, times when everything seems to be stacked against us, are not without their positive uses. When we look back after such a period, we may well wonder how on earth we ever got through. But we got through because it was our soul's purpose to do so, to face the challenge head-on, see it for what it was, and rise to the occasion. These struggles define us – make us who we are – just as the grit in the oyster shell produces the pearl. True success is nothing to do with how much money we have, or whether we are the proud possessor of the latest gismo or gadget. It is measured in *how* we use the gift of time that has been given to us to spend here on earth.

So, learning to question what is going on in your mind – and life – is a *very* healthy state to find yourself in. Once we decide that for every negative, there is a positive, we will learn to make the kind of choices that will not produce more pain and suffering for ourselves or for those who share our lives; and we will cease to snarl up our inner space with unhelpful thoughts and feelings.

When we take time to think about it, we will realise that nothing truly positive happens by dwelling in the past. Change can only come about in the present moment. Likewise, nothing ever happens by dwelling on the future. Whatever we want to happen can only happen in the present moment. I would so like to implant the idea that all grudges, resentment, bitterness and regrets stem from too much dwelling in the past; and many of our worries, stress and anxiety are caused by too much dwelling on the future.

To reach a state of mind, where we can cast off any negatives that have been engendered by dwelling too much in the past or future, is not as difficult as we may think – and I know, from personal experience, that any efforts made in this direction can bring about a profound inner transformation. All it takes to make an inroad into changing this situation is, first, to appreciate that we have a choice; and, second, to repeat as often as we remember when we are feeling got at or low: 'Nothing and nobody can make me negative. We are all masters of our own destiny.'

This kind of positive thinking *really* works. We *can*, we will discover, *rewrite* our sentence(s) and disperse those words that keep us bound mentally, emotionally and spiritually, and we can set ourself free from any thoughts or ideas that enslave and limit us!

Self-healing, then, is not only possible, it is do-able within our own homes and surroundings and it need only subtract a few minutes from our busy lives. Last thing at night, for example, before we drift into sleep, and first thing in the morning before we climb out of bed, we can remain lying flat on our back with our eyes closed. Next we can focus our attention on different parts of our body, starting with our feet (sensing each toe), then hands (sensing each finger and thumb), then legs, arms, chest, and so on. Having felt the life that exists within each part of ourself, we can, just for a minute or so, let our attention flow like an incoming tide from our feet to our head and back again.

If, at any time, we find ourself experiencing difficulty remaining in touch with our body, we can focus on our breathing. Becoming aware of this by giving attention to each inhaled breath as it enters and is then exhaled is a widely used form of meditation that has the power to centre the mind, calm you down, and bring you to stillness.

Likewise, closing the eyes and seeing ourself surrounded by a brilliant light that enters and fills our body is a very uplifting experience that can put us in touch with our own body and centre us. The important thing is not to get so attached to a thought or visual image that you remain *unattached* from your own body! The above exercises, by the way, can also be done as a natural pause and centre-ing during the day while lying on a floor or sofa.

The mind, then, assisted by our five senses, is a truly creative instrument when put to good, positive use. But if left unbridled it can become identified with a mish-mash of ideas that can create a block and get in the way of us forming true relationships with other people, with nature and with God, the Great Spirit. We can then begin to forget that, despite all the multitude of forms that exist in creation, we are in truth part of the whole – and, in reality, one with all that is.

When we stop aimless or harmless thinking by use of the methods outlined above, a space is created in the stream of thought and we experience brief moments of joy and a deep sense of harmony and peace. For those brief moments we live in the 'now' and are at our most aware and receptive and, therefore, connected to the eternal spark within us.

And, if on occasions we wake up to the fact that half the day has gone while we have been lost in thoughts which have been running round and round in circles, all we need to do is remind ourselves that all is not lost. Even when the sky is black, overcast and glowering, the sun has not given up the ghost and disappeared altogether. It is still there, as bright as ever, above or behind the clouds – and so it will be for all eternity! The same, in truth, applies to us when we are overcast – and downcast!

Whatever our situation, then – and I never forget that life can be distressingly painful and challenging for some of us – it is still within our power to tap into life-enhancing, transforming moments that will help us to cope and evolve and grow at a spiritual level.

Communication is at the heart of my work – and this book – and learning how to embrace eternity by stepping into the present moment and truly listening is also a vital step to making contact with our relatives, friends and colleagues both in this world and the next. So, never let us underestimate the value of learning how to remain anchored in the present moment.

I quite often meet people who mention that they have a very strong desire at times to give up work – and sometimes even their partners and families! – so that they be free of everyday cares and run away in search of peace and spiritual fulfilment. I understand only too well how they feel, but running away from problems is *not* the answer. If we do that, I believe that the same set of circumstances will have to be faced again, either in this life or the next. It is, I have learned, much better to 'seize the day' and face up to what is troubling us and getting in the way, and gradually accepting that the way to freedom is to bring love into all that we do.

It is, in other words, my belief that each and every one of us arrives in this world complete with an individual blueprint for the life we will lead while here on earth; and this blueprint includes certain things that we need to accomplish to enable our soul to grow. I call this 'our soul's purpose', and I believe that we set ourselves certain aims even before we are born that enable us to fill in the gaps that were not filled in during our previous life and other past incarnations.

This is not to say that we do not have free will and choices to make. These still come into play in the way we handle everything that comes our way – how we react to life in general, what we say in certain situations, who we choose to give our love to and how forgiving we are. This is where free will and choice comes in. That aside, whether we like it or not, I believe our life will start at A and end at Z – no matter how many letters we leave out in between, or how many times we return to the same comfortable letter!

I find it both comforting and challenging to know that we have a life path that is there for the taking, and a whole host of experiences ahead that will sometimes send us soaring sky-high with happiness and, at other times, test our resolve to the limits. I also believe, whether any one moment, day or year, brings us comfort or a new challenge, we have the inner resources and ability to cope and overcome trials and tribulations. If, for example, we help ourselves by just taking a moment out to listen to that inner voice and respond to the intuition that is within us all, we will find it easier to keep to our life's path and soul's purpose, and we will succeed in what we have set out to achieve.

And, whether we know it or not, we also have spirit guides and guardian angels working alongside side us in an endeavour to keep us on the straight and narrow. Once again, it is a case of taking time out from our usual circling thoughts to listen to their subtle influences as they walk beside us through life's challenges. It is only if we ignore that all-important inner voice and refuse to acknowledge the help and guidance available to us that we stray from our life's path and begin to live a life of disharmony that prevents us from learning the lessons we are here to learn. There is a whole other world out there, a wealth of spiritual knowledge and guidance for us to tap into if we only take the time.

Likewise, if we cease to take our responsibilities as a human being seriously – and lose touch with our spiritual side – we place ourselves at risk of being left at the mercy of the more unpleasant side of human nature; our own and other people's. If we pause for a moment, however, and consider what may, as a result, come our way in the next life, then maybe we will think again and not be so materialistic or violent or aggressive; and perhaps we will be kinder to each other and to animals, birds and other creatures, and begin to appreciate nature and all that it has to offer. Hopefully, too, we will be more tolerant and accepting of each other and celebrate our differences rather than allowing them to separate us and cause divisions.

Have you ever met someone with whom you feel an instant bond, as if you had known each other for years? Has a person ever come into your life just at the right moment? Has an opportunity ever come your way seemingly out of the blue and opened doors and set a whole chain of events into action? The answer is surely *yes*, and such events, I believe, are linked to our soul's purpose, and part of our life's path. Coincidence is never really coincidental, everything happens for a reason; and that reason, I believe, serves a purpose in our life and brings new opportunities for us to progress and grow.

Quite often during recent years I have been taken aback by the wisdom of the young people who attend my spiritual development seminars and workshops. The amount of understanding they have from the start is sometimes staggering. It is as if many of them, who have set their hearts on this particular path, have been born with an innate knowledge and understanding of all things spiritual. Even many children nowadays seem to have a natural acceptance that we do not die; that there is far more to humans than just a physical body.

I have now been enquiring into matters of the spirit for nineteen years and I have devoted a large proportion of my life to reading books, attending meetings and working on my own development as a medium. Even so, I do not, by any means, have all the answers to life and the afterlife; in fact, sometimes it seems that the more answers I find, the more questions I have, which is why it is always such a joy to pool knowledge with others who are on the same path.

I cannot envisage a time when I will have learned all that there is to learn. All I know is that something new seems to present itself whenever I am least expecting it! For example, I have experienced premonitions – sensing that something is about to happen *before* it happens – several times during my working life; and I have discovered that because these occur, the following question arises in many people's minds: 'Are disasters pre-ordained events that arise from the will of God?'

That is *not*, however, what I believe. I believe that, along with everything else, God created Natural Law and that Natural Law, glorious though it is most of the time, can sometimes result in a clash of elements – fire, air wind, water – too much of this, too little of that, and for a time things can become unbalanced, unstable, then erupt and create a domino effect that is beyond man's control.

This takes us back to personal responsibility. Drought, for example, can create terrible heartbreaking famines, but sometimes more than a lack of water is involved in this. Logging for commercial purposes – cutting down too many trees and hedgerows – which enables the wind to remove the earth's top soil that is vital for crops, is one example. Creating global warming, which is such a topical subject right now, is another. Scientists have found similar explanations – some *man-made* – for other 'natural' disasters.

No, I do not see any of these disasters as the wilful acts of a malevolent God, wreaking havoc on mankind. I see them as the natural – or unnatural – effects of Natural Law, many of which stem from our neglect or misunderstanding of our environment, and the awful consequences that may result from it.

Why the spirits sometimes allow a premonition of a disaster and at other times do not, I cannot explain. Perhaps one day, all will be revealed to me and I will be able to add more on this subject. Meanwhile, I can only repeat that I know, from personal experience, that premonitions do exist.

In the middle of November 2004, for example, I was subjected to one of these while I was giving a demonstration of trance mediumship to a group of students during a teaching weekend at the Arthur Findlay College in Stansted, Essex.

Trance is when a medium slips into an altered state of consciousness, so that the spirits can control the medium's mind and speak their own words and communicate more directly with those present. The actual trances vary from a 'light trance', in which the medium remains fully aware of what is being said, to a 'deep trance' in which the medium is totally unaware, oblivious to anything that is happening, including what is being said.

On the occasion at the Arthur Findlay College I was in a deep trance and therefore knew nothing about what was happening at the time. When I came out of the trance, however, I learned that the group had been warned that a terrible disaster was about to befall human beings.

Apparently, my demonstration had started normally enough with an address from my spirit guide, Zintar, which included invitations from him and Star, my other guide, to those present to receive personal spirit messages. This was quite a usual happening in a demonstration of trance, and the students in attendance, who had seen me work in this way before, thought the remainder of the demonstration would then follow the now-familiar routine, and finish with their relatives endeavouring to show themselves through transfiguration, a very evidential moment when a spirit transplants the physical features of his or her face over the medium's face. On this occasion, however, the spirit world had a very important message to relay, suddenly becoming very grave and serious, they announced that they had something 'very important to share with everybody'.

What was then said caused quite a stir in the group, but of course, it did not at that moment make a great deal of sense to the people present. Later, though, on 3 January 2005, Marilyn Pither from Portugal, a student on that weekend course and an observer of this particular trance demonstration, wrote:

I have been recalling Tony Stockwell's trance demonstration at Stansted Hall in November last year. Tony's guides came through, addressing us as they usually do, but the main difference during that sitting was that at one stage his guide became very serious and said that there would be a huge disaster and many thousands of people would be catapulted to spirit before the year was through. I was sitting at the back of the library, and when the demonstration finished I talked to another student, Julie Knowlton, and we were both disturbed by what had just been said. In all the demos I had seen Tony do in the past I had never heard anything quite like that before. Then, after the tsunami occurred on Boxing Day, it did seem that we had witnessed an extremely sad prediction.

Nicola Howell from Essex, another student who attended that weekend, wrote:

I can remember it all so clearly! During the trance, Zintar said there would be a 'catastrophic event which would catapult thousands of men, women and children from this plane to the next'. He also said that the world would 'never be the same again'. At the time this was very disturbing to hear and, as the trance demonstration came to a close, many of the sitters were discussing what had been said and were asking Tony questions. But Tony was totally unaware of what had come through him during the trance.

When Nicola heard the devastating news of the South East Asia tsunami, which had claimed so many lives on Boxing Day, she telephoned her friend, Gail, who had also been present during the November weekend. When Gail came to the phone she knew, even before Nicola said a word, *why* Nicola had telephoned her. She had already made the same connection with Zintar's prediction and the events that had just happened.

Another student, Carol Stirling from Scotland, wrote the following in January 2005:

I was very shocked when I heard the reports of the tsunami which hit South East Asia because I knew in my mind that I had heard talk of such a tragedy before it happened. Then I recalled the Trance and Physical

Mediumship course I had attended at Stansted Hall in November. This involved a session with Tony Stockwell who had done a demonstration of trance mediumship. I had been lucky to see Tony in trance before and I was, therefore, familiar with his guides Zintar and Star. When they came through on this occasion, however, I was amazed at the amount of information they were giving out. I had always been told that, while you are developing working with spirits, you are not supposed to predict, so I was shocked at the information I was hearing. By then, I had been studying trance, long and hard, for many years, and I can honestly say I had never before heard such clear definite information being given out.

The words I recall hearing were the spirit guides describing a 'terrible natural disaster which would involve thousands of innocent men, women and children being sacrificed'. The guides described the victims being 'catapulted into the spirit world', and I recall them saying this would happen before the New Year. It was an amazing amount of knowledge to be given and, for me, it has confirmed that we should always listen with open ears, minds and hearts!

I am grateful to all the students for sharing the above observations. All I can remember about that demonstration is that it was a very deep level of trance, which is unusual for a public event outside my own home circle of regular sitters.

As the demonstration came to an end, and the guides withdrew, I remember becoming conscious of my surroundings in the library at Stansted and realising that the atmosphere in the room was very tense. I had very little recollection though of what the guides had spoken about during the demonstration, and no memory at all of them passing on information about an impending disaster. What they had said only became apparent when I gave the students a chance to ask me questions about my trance mediumship. Usually at such moments, I get questions about my guides and their own development, but on this occasion the questions were all concerned with the prediction that they had just heard Zintar make.

I must confess I was a little uneasy when I heard about this. I do not usually go in for predictions – foretelling future events – in my clairvoyance work, let alone my trance mediumship. And I have always been rather sceptical about psychics, who announce after an event, that they knew it was coming! On such occasions, it is natural for people to think: 'Oh, *really*, so why didn't you do something about it then?'

More than anything, I believe that a medium's chief purpose in life is to prove that we survive death and that there is an afterlife. I also believe that mediums should be open to the influences of the great teachers and guardians in the other world, so that they can pass on great philosophies and knowledge for the benefit of all.

I do not believe that mediums exist to forecast what the future may have in store for us or to give us 'Agony Aunt' type advice. Having said that, the spirits do offer us such information sometimes.

All I can surmise from the predictions I have been given about disasters, is that we are *not* given exact place names, dates and times, because what is required of us is *not* action, but an awareness of what is to be and prayer. I know in horrific events, such as the Boxing Day tsunami, this is *very* hard to accept, especially if you have lost somebody in the tragedy. But for reasons unknown to me Zintar didn't pass on sufficient information about when and where, during the trance, to enable me to give anybody an advance warning.

To be given prophetic information from the spirit world, but not to be able to avert the terrible loss of life haunts me and is something I find very hard to handle. I can only add that I do not, by any means, have all the answers. I only wish I did.

I remember feeling similarly helpless one day in 2004, when I was on my way to do a demonstration in Swindon. While on board the tour bus that was taking me there, I fell fast asleep. In the front was the driver, John, and his wife, who had come to attend the demo. As I started to surface from this deep, fitful sleep, I realised I was crying out even before I had fully come round.

'John . . . Oh, John,' I heard myself saying. 'I've just had the most horrible vision and it's left me with the most *awful* feeling.'

'What's the matter, mate?' he asked concerned, pulling over to the side of the road.

'It's something to do with a school in Russia,' I said. 'All the children are in terrible danger.'

There was nothing John could do, of course, but placate me and wait until I calmed down.

Later, because this incident was still very fresh in my mind, I decided to mention it at the demonstration that evening, which was attended by about a thousand people.

'Do me a favour,' I pleaded. 'Earlier today, on my way here, I fell asleep and had a *horrible* vision about some children in Russia, whose lives are going to be in great danger. I don't know any more than that, but I would like you all to send them your prayers.'

Three days later the newspaper coverage and television news were full of reports concerning militants, with explosives strapped to their bodies, who had stormed a school in Beslan,

North Ossetia, a Russian region bordering Chechnya. Having gained access to the school, they had corralled hundreds of hostages – many of them children and their teachers – into a gymnasium and were threatening to blow up the building if the Russian troops, who had surrounded the school, attacked. When the troops began the rescue operation over 300 were killed, including many children.

There are so many times when we see terrible things happening around the world – and much closer to home – when we cannot help wondering and crying out in anguish: 'Where was God?' or 'Why did the Great Spirit let this happen?'

I have cried out in this way so many times myself. It's very hard not to, especially when an horrific event involves the young and innocent. Yet, each time I come back to the belief that he/she was present with them in their hour of need; and that one of the greatest gifts we are given is the gift of free will – even if it is a two-edged sword which enables the wicked to perpetrate terrible deeds. If we were not so empowered with free will, I remind myself, we would be like puppets on a string, operated by a great puppet master in the sky and that is *not* how I see God, the Great Spirit or even, despite everything, *how* I would wish things to be.

I honestly believe that the reason spirits give us advance warnings that some terrible man-made madness is about to happen, is so that we and others can join forces with our creator and help those in need by remembering them in our prayers. The power of prayer, they are suggesting, is far more powerful than we can ever know.

If we accept that there is a spirit universe – a collective consciousness belonging to the spirit mind – then we can also accept that the spirits are able to break through to us in our much denser physical world. Then, having tuned into our earth energy, they can ask us to give them our concentrated thought in prayer which enables them to do so much more for people who find themselves in terrible trouble here on earth. I find the thought of our energy blending with theirs to go to the aid of those who are in dire need deeply reassuring and comforting.

On yet another occasion, I awoke early one morning with a terrible sense of foreboding, like a great weight resting on my mind. Unusually for me, I found it *very* difficult to settle down to anything, including my breakfast.

'What's going on?' I kept asking myself. 'What *is* this sense of dread?'

Eventually, still feeling very unsettled and disturbed, I switched on the radio, just in time to hear a news flash. Bombs had gone off, almost in unison, the announcer said, at the underground stations of Aldgate East, Kings Cross and Edgware Road – and a number thirty bus that was going from Marble Arch to Hackney Wick had had its top blown off in Tavistock Square.

As the information continued to flow through and the numbers of dead and injured began to emerge, I understood *why* I had woken up with such a sense of dread and foreboding. Heartbroken for the victims and the families and friends who were now left to mourn their loss, I began to wing prayers up into the ether to help the victims cross over and to soothe the hearts of those who were left grieving, or out of their minds with worry about loved ones who were still missing.

There are moments in life when all that we can do is offer up prayers for those whose lives have been so cruelly cut short, for those who have been maimed, for their relatives and friends who are left bewildered and shocked by such a wicked premeditated act, and hope and pray, against all odds, that such a horror will never happen to anybody, anywhere, ever again.

If there is a good that comes out of these catastrophic events it is the knowledge that 'no man is an island', that for those terrible moments at least nations come together in their sense of outrage, shock and outpouring of grief; and that a stranger's loss is *our* loss, their anguish *our* anguish.

We are, in other words, intrinsically linked, intertwined, undivided – *united*. And while we can *feel* that much for each other and for people we have never met, there is still hope for us all. Good will triumph over evil. At the darkest moment there is the promise of daylight. Light will banish darkness. And the further we travel down this road, the more we will begin to understand that the veil between the two worlds is not as dense or as final, as we once believed; that with the help of the spirits and our loved ones who have passed over, it can be penetrated, can be lifted, and we can be reunited, and continue to unravel our soul's purpose.

8

Love Conquers all

Like most mediums, I am often asked if it is possible to call up anybody I want to from among the so-called dead. 'Can you get hold of Elvis for me?' young wits ask, grinning. I have also been asked to summon up: Frank Sinatra, Dusty Springfield and many other family favourites. And, sorry though I am to disappoint people, I have to reply: 'That is *not* how it works. Mediums cannot "call up" spirits on demand. Mediumship is not a one-way process that is as simple as dialling a living person on the telephone! It is a two-way process. There needs to be a personal reason – a strong bond of love and affection – for a spirit to wish to make contact with somebody here on earth.'

Famous people do come through, of course, if they have a personal need to contact somebody and, when they do, even I may not realise who they are – or just how famous or infamous they were when alive. One such situation arose, when I had no idea how famous the person was until almost the end of the reading, when I was reading for Pat Andrews, a slim, red-haired, middle-aged lady, who had a delightfully warm, chatty, bubbly personality. I could tell immediately I set eyes on her that she had led a very 'with it', somewhat colourful lifestyle, and I liked her very much.

When Pat asked to come and visit me in London for an initial reading for *Psychic Detective*, I had gone through the usual routine of asking the production team to keep me completely in the dark. This meant that before I met her I knew nothing of who she was or why she was coming to see me. That's how I wanted it. A clean slate, I believed, would clear the way for more effective communication.

When we did meet, having closed my eyes and focused, I very quickly got a strong sense that it was a young man who was trying to connect with me. I asked Pat tentatively whether someone very close to her had passed, and whether he had a great love of music and was connected to the theatre or the music world. 'Would he have had any connections with guitar music – on the radio or in records? The guitar seems to be *very* important to him. In fact, did he play the guitar in his lifetime?'

Pat, looking astonished, replied: 'Yes, he did.'

'Thank goodness for that!' I said, relieved, adding: 'As this young fella comes to me, I don't want to call him a hippie, but I feel he had his own agenda in life. Nothing fazed him . . . Likewise, I don't want to paint you as a mad-cap teenager, but you were a *very* extroverted, lively person.'

Despite her grief, Pat couldn't help smiling at this, but I could tell that, true to her instructions, she was determined not to give anything away.

'Did he mix with the kind of people who smoked marijuana?' I asked. 'I'm getting the feeling he was rather partial to it.'

Pat, looking somewhat sombre and speaking very quietly, just said: 'Yes.'

'I think this man was known by a lot of people . . . and that he was well thought of . . .' I could tell from Pat's expression that this was true and, feeling encouraged, I paused and closed my eyes to listen some more. 'Do you know if he ever went to New York?' I said, opening my eyes and looking across at Pat, who was nodding.

'Yes, he did,' she replied.

'Well, he's talking about that trip – saying something about he thought he was a bird while he was there, thought he could fly. That's a bit of a funny thing for him to say.'

Pat shook her head: 'No, *I* can understand that.'

'His life, he is telling me, was destined to be short, but unusual – *glamorous*.' I paused. 'He keeps telling me how beautiful he thinks you are . . . And that during the time you knew him, he also thought you were *very* beautiful, then.'

Tears had sprung into Pat's eyes and I paused while she regained her composure.

'I think your young man was well-known and well respected, that he performed in a band. And I think the band, and the other members of it, were very important to him.' I paused. 'Do you know if he was particularly keen on John Lennon's music.'

'Yes, he was,' Pat replied, choked.

'I ask because I strongly believe that he has now met up with John Lennon in the spirit world.' There were so many new impressions reaching me, I hardly knew which one to follow. 'The number twenty-seven is connecting with me now. Is this an age? A number of a door? Does that mean anything to you?'

Pat, back to sounding astonished, replied: '*Yes*, it does.'

I paused, withdrawing my attention from the spirit world and focusing it instead on Pat.

'At this stage of the reading,' I said, smiling. 'I need to know how I am doing. So will you give me some feedback?'

'Certainly,' Pat replied. 'You've been spot-on for a lot of things.' She paused, collecting her thoughts, then added: 'I'm here today because I'm trying to get some information about someone who was very close to me who passed over very suddenly. I have no knowledge of *how* he passed over, and I'm trying to get some idea of what happened to him. When he passed, he was twenty-seven, so that's why that number was significant.'

Pleased that the reading was going so well, I closed my eyes and re-focused on the spirit world. A moment later I asked: 'Had he been ill when he died? I am now seeing vomit – and I feel as if I am stuck in a room in a house. Does that make sense?'

Pat, gasping: 'Yes, a great deal of sense.'

'Do you know whether he was on some kind of medication before he passed? He's talking about tablets and being indoors . . . And now he's looking at some stairs in a hallway. This scene seems to be important to him. Did someone hear him calling out before he passed?'

'I don't know. I wasn't there.'

'Well, I don't think he was on his own when he died. I am getting the feeling that there were four or five people in the house.' I hesitated, concentrating even harder. 'I feel that there may well have been a party . . . alcohol . . . music . . . There's something sexual . . . something to do with someone fancying someone else. This man is a *very* sensitive man.' I paused again. 'He's making it clear you understood him, and he wants to thank you. Would it be fair to say that he wasn't exactly the conventional type?

Pat, smiling at the memory. 'That's right.'

The pleasant thoughts were short-lived, and I seemed to be entering a darker stage of the reading.

'I am now getting the sense that he was only partly dressed as he passed to the spirit world.'

'I really don't know about that.'

Having listened again, I continued: 'This is *not* a recent passing. If he was alive, he would be the same age as you are now. It's such a shame you couldn't grow old together. I'm getting the sense I need to go back in time.' I paused, then added: 'I am seeing newspaper cuttings, lots of them.' I paused again, reluctant to pass on what I was now seeing, but feeling I must. 'Was there blood when he passed? I can see blood and puncture wounds on his body. And now I am smelling something – something that smells like burning petrol. I think someone is burning the evidence. Do you understand any of this?'

Pat, looking incredibly sad. 'Yes, I can understand why they might do that.'

'There was someone else, too, a silent witness, watching from a window, who was too scared to say anything, who has never spoken up.' I paused again. 'I keep going into a cellar. Why might that be?'

Pat, looking and sounding unsure: 'I don't believe there was a cellar, but I know one of rooms in the house had a lowered floor.'

'Were drug dealers involved?'

'Possibly, yes.'

Feeling drained, I added: 'The only other thing I want to say to you right now is that when I said this person knew a lot of people, I think it was because he, himself, was famous.'

Pat, who had now lowered her guard, nodded and replied: 'You are right.'

'He keeps wanting to sing to you.' I paused, surprised at what I had just picked up. 'Did he meet John Lennon and Elvis Presley?' Then, as Pat smiled and nodded, I said: 'Okay, Pat, at this stage, I need to know from you how I am doing and if I'm being effective.'

'You've been spot-on again,' Pat replied, unable to resist a grin that spread from ear to ear. 'The person is *Brian Jones*, of the Rolling Stones. So, you were correct in almost everything you said.' She paused, her expression returning to its customary sadness, then added: 'I've never had a reading with a medium before but I decided that it was worth a try. At the very least, it was a different approach, one that I felt couldn't do any harm.'

I sat there a moment, recalling the 1960s and conjuring up what I remembered about the young Rolling Stones. I must admit I have never been into rock or pop music, preferring the swing music of Frank Sinatra and other crooners, but I did, of course, know of the Rolling Stones and their music. Destined to become one of the biggest stars of the 1960s, Brian Jones had attracted scores of screaming fans and caused a lot of controversy during his short life as an anti-establishment hero. When he was found dead at a tragically young age a verdict of 'death by misadventure' had been brought in, but plenty of insiders had continued to air their belief that they suspected foul play.

'All I want to know,' Pat said, her expression one of deep sorrow, 'is *how* Brian died. That's what keeps me going, and I will keep on going until I find the answer.' She paused to brush tears from the corner of her eyes. 'When Brian was found dead, nobody bothered to do much of an investigation, and his death was left as an open verdict. And, ever since then I have been trying to get to the truth.'

'The truth,' I said as gently as I could, given what I was about to say, 'is that Brian was murdered – and it all had something to do with a betrayal.'

'I have *always* believed he was murdered,' Pat replied, her voice breaking. 'But I had no way of moving forward.'

My reading had confirmed Pat's worst suspicions, and I was also aware that the insights that had come through from the spirit world had set my own investigations on a collision course with the official verdict of 'death by misadventure'.

All Pat's responses were very encouraging. Without any prior knowledge of her or Brian's life, I had succeeded, with the help of the spirits, in identifying the man she had wanted to connect with and also made some intriguing connections with the known facts of Brian's death. But could I now address the question of *how* he actually died?

'Pat, can I ask you how you were connected to Brian?' I said gently.

'We met in Cheltenham when we were teenagers,' she replied. 'After we had our son, Julian Mark, we came up to London together. So, I was with Brian before he was a Rolling Stone, at the very beginning of his career.'

Pat was only too happy to talk to me about her life with Brian and told me that, when she discovered she was pregnant with Brian's child, in 1961, it was a very difficult time for them as young unmarried parents. But it had its good moments, too. When Pat was recuperating in hospital after the birth of their son, Mark, she was, she told me, in for a very pleasant surprise.

'I saw this big bunch of flowers and a pair of feet walking into the ward,' she said. 'And I thought: "I wonder who those are for?" Then, all of a sudden, I saw Brian's face peep round the side of the flowers. If I hadn't been tucked in to the bed, I would probably have fallen out. Brian, bless him, had sold a number of his treasured albums to buy the flowers for me.'

Soon after this, however, Brian, ever restless, was on the move. Fired by his dream to take his guitar playing to another level, the music scene in London was beckoning him and he responded. Pat followed with Mark, and was there to witness his early attempts at forming a band.

She told me, 'Brian was working and also putting adverts in all the musical papers for musicians, and then auditioning them in the hope of getting a band together. All the hard work began to pay off as he gathered musicians together and gave them the name, the Rolling Stones.' She paused, needing a moment to control the tears brought on by these reminiscences. 'I sat here today trying to remain composed, but you came so close it was almost scary and part of me didn't want to believe what you were saying, what I was hearing.'

As soon as she had regained her composure I decided that now was the moment to end the reading, which had obviously been very emotional for her. It had not been an easy reading for me either. I had realised fairly early on that the spirit I was in touch with was a blond, multi-talented musician, with green-grey eyes, who had attempted but failed to juggle the use of drugs with his musical output.

I was also aware that, although the coroner had recorded an open verdict after he was found drowned at the bottom of his swimming pool, the actual circumstances of his death had left many unanswered questions and had remained highly controversial. Given how distressing all of this must have been for Pat, who was the mother of his son, I had taken pains throughout the reading to proceed very cautiously.

As Pat and I said our goodbyes, we agreed that we would continue to work together and travel back to some of the places that had been important to her and Brian.

When I was speaking to Pat she was very reassuring about how many accurate details my reading had contained. Then, putting on a very brave face, she said: 'I realise that we will probably never get to the bottom of what happened to Brian the night that he died. But at least you were able to confirm what I had always felt, that his death was not an accident. Even getting this far, which is further than I had dreamt of when I came to see you, has brought about some closure and really has been a life-changing experience for me. It was so wonderful for me to receive Brian's message and to realise that he still remembers the people he loved. He was a very special man, who lived the short life he had to the full, and at least those of us who loved him can be glad and celebrate that.'

According to the official statements there were three people with Brian on the evening he died – three people who, at some point, had all gone off to do separate things, leaving Brian alone in the pool. When they came back they said they found him in the pool 'incapacitated'. Having pulled him out, however, they discovered that he was dead.

The mental images that I had seen, though, were miles away from what was said at the time and the official verdict. They were however similar, I learned later, to ideas that had been expressed by a number of people who had conducted investigations into the circumstances surrounding Brian's death. So, at least, I was not alone in going out on a limb by rejecting the official verdict of 'death by misadventure'. Having done that, however, I now had to investigate my own controversial ideas in more detail; and this began with Pat taking me back to Cheltenham where she and Brian had grown up and where they had first met as teenagers on a blind date.

'I was quite taken with this angelic-looking young man with shiny blond hair!' Pat told me as we walked to the first-floor flat, near the town centre, where Brian had been living during that time.

Fortunately having persuaded the present owners to let us spend some time inside, we found ourselves standing in what had once been Brian's bed-sitting-room.

'Of course there were always parties here,' Pat said, grinning. 'I guess word just got around that this was THE place to be. It was always buzzing. I remember Brian coming into the kitchen during a party here, and sitting at the table playing his guitar. He played and he played and didn't stop until his fingers started to bleed.'

As Pat was talking, I was standing there hoping that this location, which had been so important to Brian, would help me pick up a spirit trail. Psychics believe that echoes of past events and personalities get mixed in with bricks and mortar.

But would Brian's bedroom, I wondered, yield any such connections? I touched the walls and tried to absorb any lingering presence. I got a strong feeling that Brian had found it hard to sleep here, that his mind was too full of dreams and plans. There was a real sense of excitement. Then he began to take my mind back to what happened when he passed.

'I'm feeling again the strong impression that there was a puncture wound in the right side of his chest; and that there was a gap of several hours before his body was discovered. I am also getting the sense that he had a premonition and that at the time he passed he kind of knew what was going to happen.'

All this new information was clearly surprising for Pat but, once we were outside the flat, she reassured me she could cope, telling me that although it had been disturbing over all she was very glad to have taken part.

A few days after our visit to Cheltenham, the *Psychic News*, under the heading, 'Rolling Stone Was Murdered', published the following:

Brian Jones, the member of the Rolling Stones who was found dead in a Sussex swimming pool in 1969, was murdered. That's the verdict of medium Tony Stockwell, whose investigation into the mystery will be screened later this year. Tony, whose *Psychic Detective* LIVINGtv programme starts a new series next month, visited Brian's old haunts in Cheltenham to try and discover the facts behind his mysterious death . . . Pat Andrews, who was Brian's girlfriend and the mother of their son 'feels the official version of how Brian died isn't the whole story, so that's what Tony's investigating'. Tony did not know who Pat was and just gave her what he got using his abilities. It was pretty amazing.

During the sitting, Tony linked with a young man who played the guitar and liked or knew John Lennon. Tony's conclusion was that Brian was murdered, but it was made to look like drowning.

'One of the major blights in my life has been never being satisfied with the verdict on Brian's death,' said Pat Andrews.

Back in London, Pat told me that Brian's first regular booking, after they arrived in the capital, was a cellar club called the Crawdaddy, which was situated under the Station Hotel in Richmond, Surrey.

When we arrived there with the film crew to continue our investigations, we discovered it was now just a storeroom. It was, nevertheless, still a place that was full of memories for Pat; and it was another chance for me to pick up on Brian's spirit trail as I continued to look into the mysterious circumstances surrounding his death.

As we entered the cellar, Pat said, that time, when Brian had just arrived in London, from Cheltenham was such a great time. 'He was chasing his dream and in fact, I think he was the happiest he had ever been then because he was doing what he wanted to do. The band was raw, but they were so good.'

Having walked through the cellar with Pat, as she told me all about how the room used to be packed with teenagers, I came to a halt at the back of the room, which I instinctively felt was the best place to try sifting through layers of time and make contact with Brian as he was then.

'I'm asking if Brian is able to manifest through me, or connect with us in this space,' I said to Pat. 'And I am getting a definite sense that Brian is with us. You know how someone puts their arm around another person's shoulders and leans up against them, that's what I feel Brian is doing to you right now

– just leaning companionably against the side of you. I also think that back in the day it would have been something of a competition as to which one of you was the prettiest! In the image you're saying, "Don't lean on me, Brian" because your clothes will be creased and Brian's saying, "Don't lean on me, Pat, because you'll crease my shirt!"'

'What I'd like to do, Pat,' I added a moment later, 'is some automatic writing.'

Having set this up, I felt my hand being guided by a spirit and, suddenly, the pen started to move so fast it came off the writing pad and began to write on the box the pad was resting on. When my hand eventually stopped moving, we were able to read the words: *I love you, let me show you the way. You were my sunshine, love my son, shine for me.*

It was a rather strange message, but one that Pat clearly found very moving.

'Just thinking back to that time and how Brian felt about me then has set my heart pounding,' she said.

It was obvious the visit was stirring up old memories for Pat – some good, some painful – and she then told me that as Brian's Crawdaddy Club days started to take off, his growing success had come at a cost to their relationship.

'At the end of 1963,' she explained, 'I had to make a choice about *how* I wanted our son to be brought up. Whether he should have what I thought of as a normal upbringing or stay in a rather unreal world. In the end, I felt that I *should* take him back to Cheltenham, which is what I did. It wasn't a decision I made lightly, though. I just felt that it was the right one for him.'

After her return to Cheltenham, Pat told me that she had to watch from the sidelines as the Rolling Stones shot to stardom and were rarely out of the headlines over the next six years, as they released eight albums and seven number one singles.

During that time Brian had become highly respected as a musician, but there was always a darker side to his fame. Having fallen prey to a series of humiliating drug-busts, his wild lifestyle affected his performances and there were clashes about musical direction. Early on, he lost his role as leader in the group and began to feel increasingly sidelined. In 1969, when he finally left the Rolling Stones, he withdrew to his country retreat, Cotchford Farm, in Sussex. Friends from those days remember he tried to remain positive and that there was even some talk of him forming a new group. A month later, however, he was found dead at the bottom of his swimming pool.

'I heard about Brian's death on the radio,' Pat told me, her voice breaking. 'And, of course, I just went into shock. I thought I had misheard and I waited by the radio for the next news to come on. When it did, it said the same thing and I was just *devastated*. I *couldn't* believe what I was hearing, especially when they said, "Death by drowning". I knew Brian was a very good swimmer, and I didn't believe for one moment that he could have died by drowning. I was in shock for an awful long time after that.'

After the official autopsy when the verdict of 'death by misadventure' was recorded, Pat was *not* the only one to suspect foul play, as I was about to discover when I met up with Trevor Hobly, a leading authority on Brian Jones, who had conducted his own meticulous investigation into the facts surrounding Brian's death.

I later heard from a man who had been involved with the case for many years. His investigations had revealed that a neighbour of Brian's had seen a bonfire outside the house on the morning that Brian's body was discovered, and people running in and out of the house. This tallied with the image of evidence being burned that I had seen during the first reading for Pat.

When I mentioned that I felt that Brian was murdered in the house, nowhere near the pool, and that I had a sense that there was a puncture wound just under the ribcage on the right-hand side of his body, I was met with astonishment. The investigator told me that there had never been any official mention of a puncture wound but that he had been told about it by a reliable witness.

Could a tiny syringe puncture wound have been missed by a pathologist investigating what seemed to be a clear case of drowning, I found myself wondering, and, if so, what role would it have played in Brian's death?

The place, I decided, that could hold the answer – and the truth about Brian's death – was Cheltenham cemetery. Brian's body, the investigator told me, had been brought there a week after he died, and it had been no ordinary burial. Decisions taken at the time meant that the body – and any hidden forensic clues – would still be remarkably preserved thirty-five years later.

Brian's body was embalmed and his hair was bleached white and apparently, he was buried in an air-tight metal casket. In addition, he was buried ten feet down, which means that his body would effectively be frozen and therefore preserved.

Having heard these macabre details, I found myself thinking that, given Brian's body would still hold the key to how he died, getting permission for the body to be exhumed and a fresh autopsy carried out, would be the only way to resolve the mystery surrounding his death.

Hoping that we could take the case to the police, I decided that now was the time for me to visit Cotchford Farm, in Sussex, the scene of Brian's death.

When, accompanied by Pat, I arrived at the house, we discovered that it was still largely as it had been in 1969 when Brian lived there, and that the swimming pool where his body was found was still in existence as a poignant reminder of his untimely death.

According to the three witnesses, who had admitted being in the house at the time, they had all had a few drinks then decided to go for a late-night swim. One by one they had left the pool until only Brian remained in the water. A short while later one of them had returned to find him at the bottom of the swimming pool. An ambulance was called, but Brian was pronounced dead on arrival at the hospital. The autopsy then revealed non-lethal but significant amounts of alcohol and drugs in his system and the cause of death was given as drowning.

Believing that the fabric of the buildings may contain some imprints and echoes of Brian's tragic death, I made the necessary preparations to draw my own psychic conclusions.

'Of course, part of me *doesn't* want to be here,' Pat said as we stood around the pool area. 'But you can't be too emotional, can you, when you are trying to get to the bottom of these sort of things. It's *very* hard, but I feel I have to do it.'

'Being here is proving to be *very* interesting,' I replied. 'When I first read for you, Pat, I picked up a number of things about Brian, but the swimming pool didn't actually figure in anything I sensed. That's interesting because I now know that the pool was thought to be involved in his death and I am trying to understand why it never came up during the reading.'

As we continued to stand by the pool, I became even more convinced that Brian's passing was the result of foul play rather than a swimming accident.

'Although I am always very careful about what I tell people,' I said to Pat, 'because I don't want to cause them more pain when they might have managed to bury some of their demons already, I do feel that this swimming pool is a kind of camouflage for what really happened. I honestly don't believe that Brian had too much to drink and then drowned. The image I'm getting, as we stand here, is that his murder was to do with a betrayal – something to do with money, material possessions – that kind of thing.' I paused, feeling the moment had come to move on. 'Let's walk around the grounds and get another view of the pool from up that slope.'

Having done that and come to a halt at the top of the grassy slope, I turned to Pat and said: 'Again, the impressions I am picking up are very interesting – and I can tell you now that, although originally I thought there was only one person involved in Brian's murder, I now know that is *not* the case. Standing here, I have a definite sense that at least two people helped to lower Brian into the pool.' I paused to check that Pat was still all right as she listened to this information then, having established she was okay, I added: 'I think our next step should be to go into the house.'

Did its walls, I wondered as we walked up to the building, witness a terrible crime – and could I use this opportunity to conduct a psychic analysis of its bricks and mortar to good effect and explain what happened?

Once inside the house, I said to Pat: 'The vibes I am picking up here are very different from those I got outside. I'm getting a very strong sense that, whatever happened to Brian, the deed itself took place *here* – *inside* the house. And I'm also sensing that *two* people were involved in the deed itself and that there were two other people lurking about outside.'

Having sat down, I re-focused my mind and went along with a stream of images. 'I'm now getting a strong sense that Brian was called into the house where a big man and a smaller man confronted him. Brian was then immobilized by an injection that contained some kind of medication that couldn't be detected after the event; and it was this injection that caused the puncture wound I saw. Then, as he slipped into a state of unconsciousness, he was taken from the house by the two men and lowered into the pool face-down. His last moments were definitely in the water.' Refocusing again, I added: 'The people who did this to him were *paid* to kill him – hired assassins.' I paused, knowing there was still more to see and to say. 'I need to establish more about the significance of there being four in the group and, to do this, I feel I need to go back to the area around the swimming pool.'

Having returned to where we had stood before, I turned to Pat and said, 'I now feel that *this* is where the other two stood watching and waiting.' I broke off for a moment, then continued: 'It's strange because I am now picking up that they were *really* sinister people, and it was *they* who had wanted the deed done. The sense of their presence is staining the whole atmosphere of this place.'

As Pat and I moved on and began to walk the path that would have been used to carry Brian from the house to the pool, I found myself wondering if, with the help of the spirits, I would now be able to fill in the details of his final moments. Then, as more impressions started to come through, I turned to Pat and said: 'Earlier on, I picked up that two people, who were lurking outside were aware of what was going on inside the house. I now feel that it was those two people who were directing what was happening.' I paused, then added: 'When Brian was brought from the house, I get the sense that the big guy was carrying him by his arms and the smaller guy was holding on to his feet, and as they got closer to the pool, the smaller guy tripped and dropped Brian before regaining his balance and helping to place him in the water to make it look like an accident. And what I strongly believe now is that, while Brian's body was being lowered into the water, there was a young woman in the house, looking out. She saw what happened but, shortly after the event, she was warned off and was left so scared she didn't dare to come forward.' I paused, turning to Pat. 'I know all this sounds very theatrical . . .'

'But sometimes truth is stranger than fiction,' Pat replied. 'And I have to say you have touched on things today that we had already considered – or found out about – and, as you couldn't have known any of this in advance, it *has* to be more than a coincidence.' She paused, then added sadly: 'I just feel that we are almost there; that we have almost reached the end of the trail.'

It was true. My psychic investigation had reached its conclusion and for Pat it was the end of a long, emotional rollercoaster day and years of longing for answers.

The following day, Pat and I met up again to reflect on the the night before. She told me that although she had been terribly upset and shaken, she felt very strongly that if the experience helped to establish the truth about Brian, then it was worth putting herself through so many difficult emotions. I was relieved because I really wasn't sure how Pat would feel. And of course it was not within my power to re-open the case officially – only the police could do that. But Pat clearly felt that the information, and the whole experience, had given her some comfort.

Soon after we had parted from each other and gone our separate ways, I learned that the results of my psychic investigation had been passed to the police in the hope that there would be moves to exhume Brian's body and re-open the case. Whether this will happen or not is out of my control, but I do hope it does for the sake of all those who loved Brian.

I had grown very fond of Pat during the time we had spent together, and I was *so* relieved that the reading – and our subsequent journeys to her and Brian's old haunts – had all worked out so well for her. Brian's life might have been short, but as a member of the Rolling Stones he had earned a place in the hearts of millions and had never lost the place he found in Pat's heart when he was a very young man.

One way and another, I felt that setting aside my doubts and taking up the challenge of using my psychic gifts for *Psychic Detective* had worked out for the best for me and for those who had been so much in need of answers about the loss of their loved one.

As far as Pat and Brian were concerned, it just remains for me to repeat something I said at the beginning of this chapter: that although mediums cannot just call up the spirits of famous or, for that matter, even so-called ordinary people, if there is a strong enough personal bond, like that which existed between Brian and Pat, spirits will put in an appearance for their loved ones. The fact remains that spirit is indestructible, whatever form its life takes!

True love, I have had confirmed time and time again in my work, is also indestructible. Those we love truly and deeply become an eternal part of us, and the longer we live the more people there will be – husbands, wives, in-laws, children and friends of friends – who will become part of our inner community, our soul group. And the wider that community becomes, the easier it will be for us to recognise our own loved ones in the eyes or gestures of complete strangers.

Love begets love. That's how love grows. So, we must never hesitate to love – and to love deeply. We might be afraid of the pain and the anguish that love can heap upon us when those we love die and leave us bereft, but *that*, heartbreaking though it is, should not be allowed to hold us back from loving. Those we love do not really depart from us. They remain part of us forever and, one day, we will be reunited.

Love, I can only emphasise, is stronger than death; and the

Great Spirit's love, which is the best love of all, was there for us before we were born while we were still being knitted in our mother's womb, and it will be there for us still when we have died, and there for us again when we are re-born! Good things happen in life, terrible things happen, unimaginable things happen. But one thing remains constant. Love is eternal and, working as it does sometimes in unseen, mysterious ways, it conquers all.

9
Time Past, Time Present

We are born and then we die – it is as *simple* as that. This is still, perhaps, one of the most common beliefs I come across. But there are other possibilities, other points of view. Some people, who believe in an afterlife, for example, also believe that when we die, we will dwell in a place where the sun always shines, the birds always sing and the flowers always bloom and permeate the atmosphere with a heavenly fragrance. And so we live in bliss *forever*. That may be a perfectly lovely belief – and one I wouldn't at all mind sharing! – but it is *not* one that I am able to go along with completely.

I believe we are born and die many times, and that each lifetime here on earth is another opportunity for us to continue learning and developing spiritually, another chance for us to nourish and enrich our body, mind and soul. I am also convinced that the sooner we embrace this view of eternity and live our lives accordingly, the better it will be for all of us.

Likewise, I am equally sure that the lessons we need to learn in each lifetime have nothing to do with the wrath of God, divine retribution, being paid back, or punished in some way for not being as good as we should have been in our previous life. The results of our actions, good, bad or indifferent, I believe, are entirely down to us.

For people who believe in karma, the most important aspect of accepting that we do not die, that there *is* an afterlife, is the knowledge that *how* we choose to live this life has a direct effect on our next life. I cannot emphasise enough, though, that I do not see this as a form of divine retribution, but as a gift in which, throughout many lifetimes, we are given free will and the opportunity to become better people and perfect our individual souls – which would indeed be bliss!

Each lifetime has its blessings and its trials and tribulations, which offer us the opportunity to progress until we realise our full potential as a human being. I have never believed in a God, who, like a puppet master, pulls our strings and determines how our life will begin, what form our body will take and how our lives will proceed and end. I believe that having been given free will, we determine our own destiny; and, if we are born into a particularly tough set of circumstances, the going may be rough and test us to our limits, but the chance to make spiritual progress and develop is still there.

Given that I have had so many personal experiences of my own past lives, it would be very difficult for me *not* to believe in reincarnation – the rebirth of my soul into a new body. One past-life occasion I vividly recall occurred very recently when I was driving alone through the meadowsweet lands of Suffolk. At one moment as I glanced through the passenger window of my car I saw in my mind's eye a huge mansion at the end of a magnificent tree-lined drive. A second later, feeling that I was about to link with one of my past-life experiences, I pulled into a nearby layby where, almost immediately, I found myself propelled back to a life I had lived in the late fifteen hundreds.

In the vision I was a young man, aged about twenty, dressed in some very fine period clothes, and I instinctively knew that I was on my way to be married to a beautiful young bride who had lovely, long, blonde hair. In my mind I knew, beyond question, that her name was Emily. The image was *so* strong, *so* powerful that I then saw myself standing alongside her in a very small chapel that had stained glass windows, and the next moment we were man and wife. There was just a handful of people present at the ceremony and I instinctively knew that the marriage was taking place in secret under the veil of darkness. The next thing I saw was myself and my new bride running, as if in fear of our life, back down the tree-lined drive towards the house; and, behind us, in hot pursuit were fearsome-looking men mounted on horseback.

What happened after that I do not know at this moment. I can only add that the vision left me feeling forlorn as if there was something missing in my life, as if something way back in time that had been left undone needed to be recognised and acknowledged to enable me to put things right.

Some hours later, although I was still in the same keyed up emotional state, I had a very real sense that, one day soon, our paths were destined to cross again. I really do believe that we can reincarnate and have relationships with the same friends, lovers and family members from one life to another.

I am not quite sure how the young lady, who was once my bride, will re-emerge in my life – or what part she might possibly play when she does – but I know I want to invite her back and resolve the outstanding issues that exist between us. Whether she will eventually return as a friend, colleague or teacher, I do not know. But I do know we will meet again.

One lovely spring afternoon I found myself reading for an attractive lady who had a very pleasant smile. Called Janice, she was in her early forties and still, as she said, 'single'. As I dipped into her energy to lift my mind to the spirit world to see if there was anybody present who was connected to her, I saw a very clear image of a pyramid. At first, I thought she had an Egyptian spirit guide who was about to come through but, no, only the image of the pyramid remained. When I passed this information on to her, she looked very intrigued and said: 'What else do you see?'

'The River Nile,' I replied. 'And a lovely cool oasis, camels, and many other sights and sounds that you would expect to find in a desert setting in Egypt.'

For a moment, I felt like apologising for what seemed to be such way-out bizarre images, but Janice was looking very happy and kept saying: 'That's *really* fascinating. What else do you see?'

As she was so responsive, I decided to dip still deeper into her energy and, as I did so, I discovered that she had always felt herself to be an outsider, a person who always seemed to be living on somebody else's margins.

'I loved my mum and dad,' she said when we were talking about this. 'But I never *really* felt I fitted in and I had exactly the same feeling about my friends. I always felt lost – disconnected – and, above all, I felt I was *searching*, constantly on the look-out for something, somebody that was missing in my life.'

'Have you heard of soul groups?' I asked.

'Yes, I have,' she replied. 'But that's as far as my knowledge goes.'

'Soul groups,' I explained, 'consist of people within the spiritual world – and within the earthly world – who, in one form or another, are closely connected to us; and who may well have been connected to us since the beginning of time. They are like-minded individuals, who are strongly linked to our soul's purpose, our mission in this life and the next and the next *ad infinitum*.'

Having paused while Janice absorbed this explanation, I then continued: 'Although you are feeling very much alone at this moment, I am receiving information that this situation is about to change; that, without a shadow of a doubt, you will be visiting Egypt one day soon and, while you are there, you will meet your soul-mate.'

I know, at one level, this all sounds terribly romantic, like something out of a Mills and Boon novel, but Janice's reaction was *very* responsive.

'There's *no* way you could have known this,' she said, a note of excitement in her voice. 'But all my life, certainly from the age of six when I first saw an illustration of a pyramid in one of my books, I have dreamed of going to Egypt. And I think one of the reasons I have never married is that I have always believed that, one day, I would travel to a far-flung exotic place and meet my soul-mate. And, hold your breath, my first choice of destination has always been *Egypt*!'

At this point, having returned to the spirits for further information, I once again saw the image of the pyramid and heard a sure steady voice booming in my ear: 'Tell her again what we wish you to tell her. Tell her she will go to Egypt where she will find her soul-mate and all will be well.'

Having given this information once more to Janice, I brought the reading to a close and she departed looking very much happier than she had looked when she first arrived.

Some months later, when I had almost forgotten this reading, I received a handwritten letter that had an Egyptian stamp and postmark. Janice, I discovered, had saved up all her annual leave and gone to Egypt on holiday.

'The first couple of weeks,' she wrote, 'were completely uneventful. But, on the very last day, when I wandered off from the small group of people I was visiting a pyramid with, and returned to a pyramid we had visited earlier, I found myself engaged in a conversation with an American. As we sat down together at the foot of the pyramid, he told me he was travelling alone around the world after separating from his partner of several years.'

Having struck up an instant friendship, Janice and the American had swopped addresses and started to correspond with each other by email. Then, because the man was so used to travelling, he had arranged to visit her on a number of occasions.

The next communication that arrived for me had a postmark I had somehow been expecting!

'Having fallen head-over-heels in love,' an ecstatic Janice informed me, 'we got married and we're now back in Egypt on honeymoon. We've *truly* found our soul-mate, and we're both convinced beyond the shadow of a doubt that we once shared another life together in this place, close to the foot of one of the pyramids. *Please* thank your spirits for us.'

I did!

Thanks to my spirit guide, Zintar, I once had what I can only describe as a very ethereal experience to do with the way in which our souls progress. This occurred one morning when I was meditating. For once, I was not plagued by the usual thoughts and distractions and I had reached a very deep level of meditation. During this state, which felt like bliss, I went from meditating to what I can only describe as an all-encompassing vision in which I had a part to play myself.

In the vision, which felt timeless, I was joined by beings from the spirit world, including my guide, Zintar. As Zintar came close to me, he indicated that he had brought another spirit along that he wished me to meet and connect with.

'The meeting with this spirit,' he said, standing to one side and letting the other being come forward, 'will enhance still further your abilities to connect and blend with us.'

The next moment I found myself joined by a being who I can only describe as truly androgenous. This took me by surprise for a moment or two, because usually when I am connecting with the spirit world I get an immediate sense of their gender, or what gender they wished to be perceived as at that time. They might show themselves as they were in their last embodiment, and this is certainly the case when they wish to be recognised by the living person they are hoping to make contact with or give a message to here on earth. At such times, they might also bring forward their personalities which, along with what makes us 'us' are not lost when we pass. Although spirits who choose to work with us have, more often than not, usually lived many lives, because they want to be recognised by their loved ones still on earth, they show themselves to us as they were in their most recent incarnation.

On this occasion, however, as I sat blending with the androgenous spirit, I had no sense whatsoever of a predominant gender. I just had this impression of a beautiful pure spirit. In my mind, I remember finding this rather strange at first and asking: 'Why do I not perceive you as a man or a woman?'

'I have worked through all my earthly incarnations,' the response came back. 'And I now live permanently here in the spirit world, where there is no need for me to present myself as male or female.'

As I stood absorbing this, the being added: 'There is a point in the soul's progression where, having lived a life as a man or a woman on many occasions, we progress and achieve a higher state where there is no need for a male or female embodiment.'

As I looked into this being's face, I was aware of the softest skin I had ever seen and an extraordinary beauty and lightness of being.

When I enquired why I had been granted the honour of meeting such a being, I was left with the sense that, just as Zintar was my spiritual guide, this being was Zintar's spiritual guide. It was as if I was being told: 'I guide your guide, therefore I am your guide, too. And beyond me, there is my guide, and so on and so forth.'

In my mind it was very much a case of: we are born, we live, we grow and, throughout countless embodiments, we develop spiritually until we become as enlightened as the enlightened ones, then we merge with and become co-creators with God.

Throughout all this, the vision remained *so* soft, *so* light and ethereal that I truly had a sense of what it was like to be in the presence of an enlightened being, who was teaching me about the soul's progression, and what it felt like to be a 'feather on the breath of God'.

I look back on that experience as one of the most beautiful experiences of my life – and one which I would be happy to re-experience any time!

What I love about the whole concept of reincarnation is that *nothing is wasted*. We do not spend our lives on earth struggling, learning and acquiring skills and talents only to peak and die and, therefore, be left with the thought: 'What a terrible waste of time and effort!' Instead, all the struggles are worthwhile and all the knowledge we have acquired and the hard-earned development of skills and talents are gathered up when we die and remain within us as a rich inheritance that can be re-evoked in our next life. We never, in other words, have to learn the same lessons twice!

'Does all this mean,' people ask, 'that things are set in stone, that our lives are pre-ordained?'

That was a question I once struggled with myself, which is why I always sympathise with those who ask it. What my spirit guides have helped me to understand, though, is that *nothing* is written in stone. We have been given free will and each time we find ourselves at a crossroads with a decision to be made, it is what we choose and what we do from that moment on that sets a train of events in motion. Each life presents us with little and big decisions and choices – and only we can make them. Some choices we make have positive results; some have negative results. Over time, we begin to know things by their 'fruits'; some leave a good taste in the mouth, so to speak, some not so good!

At the same time, it is certainly true that some people have a strong sense of purpose, vocation, or mission from their earliest years but, in a sense, whether we are aware of it or not, we all do! We are all reborn here on earth to achieve something and, however long any particular achievement takes, is entirely up to us.

Another question that crops up from time to time is: 'If we reincarnate, does that mean that my loved one will be back here on earth by the time I pass, and that I will not see them in the spirit world?'

My response to this is: 'I quite understand that this is the kind of thinking that makes some people feel very uncomfortable about the concept of reincarnation. Nobody wants to think that their mother or father, brother or sister, son or daughter has been reborn and is living again somewhere on earth while they are still grieving for and missing them terribly. But that is *not* how I believe things work. I believe that this is where the concept of 'soul groups' comes into play; and that, within a larger time frame, we may all be reincarnated with those who were our family, friends and colleagues here on earth.

It could be said that we have 'earned' each other and that the choice we have as individuals is whether we bring out the best or the worst in those who share our lives. There are, of course, exceptions. Not everyone who crosses our path becomes – or remains – part of our soul group and, given how many people we come into contact with on a daily basis, this is hardly surprising! I remain sure, however, that in one way or another, through this or that person, we are all connected to everybody else on the planet.

It could also be said that some people come into our life for a short time in order to impart something that will help us with our journey. The fact that they disappear from our life as quickly and as easily as they came into it, does not mean that we have failed. We just need to accept that this was meant to be, and that there will always be some people who come and go and who remove themselves from our lives – and some people we remove ourselves from! This is doubtless because we have learned what we need to learn from them and now is time to move on. Likewise, we need to have faith in the fact that those who remain with us are meant to be with us; that they are part of our soul group and are the ones with whom we shall go on to have many more experiences.

This brings us to the next question: 'What happens to evil people and all manner of wretches who enter other people's lives and do them harm? Are truly wicked people, like Hitler and other tyrants, who have committed terrible atrocities on mankind, punished in the afterlife?'

I do not believe that there is a punishment block in the higher realms, or that God, the Great Spirit, is there to make evil people suffer by handing out divine retribution in the form of terrible punishments – the so-called 'fires of hell and damnation'. I believe such people, who have so abused and misused their free will decide their own fate and that they will, in the afterlife, find themselves in the company of other like-minded spirits. In other words, I believe that the Law of *like to like* comes into effect here and, that wrongdoers of every description will, sooner or later, find themselves among a group of wrongdoers. I also believe that they will have to re-live their rotten deeds, both in the sense of a replay of their wrongdoing; or actually experiencing themselves, in one lifetime or another, the misery they have inflicted on others. Such people, I believe, escape nothing and they may, during a series of rebirths, have to live through some of the atrocities they put their victims through. '*Do unto others as you would have done unto yourself*' is a wonderful guide-line to live by.

The concept of *like to like* is yet another example of why accepting that there is an afterlife and karma has such a direct profound and practical effect on *how* we choose to live our lives and *how* we treat others.

The expression 'Jesus wept' seems to me to be so apt for horrendous, heartbreaking, tragic situations and I am sure that all the innocent victims who are caught up in such events will be taken care of in a very special way.

'Are the relationships within a soul group,' I am asked, 'always the same? Is a son always a son, a sister a sister, for example?'

Again, as I understand it, the relationships within a soul group are *fluid* and may vary from one lifetime to another. It also makes sense of those moments when we think we are meeting somebody for the first time, yet have the feeling that we have met before or feel that we have known each other all our lives. The truth is doubtless that we have – and we have just re-met one of our soul-mates!

At the end of the day, whether or not we believe in reincarnation and karma, it is good to think on these things. We may never find all the answers we seek in any one lifetime, but as the wise are so fond of saying, and I am so fond of quoting: 'every journey begins with one step'! I am an ordinary man, blessed with an extraordinary gift, and it is my belief that if I am able to summon up the *will* and the *curiosity* to take the first step towards pondering on such things, anyone can do the same!

10
Comings and Goings

People never cease to be fascinated by the idea of mediums going into a trance and surrendering themselves to the higher mind of their spirit guides. In part, I think this is because trance has had so many starring roles in old spooky films! In reality though, as I mentioned earlier, trance is when a medium slips into an altered state of consciousness, so that the spirits can communicate more directly. This state can best be described as the blending of two minds, the mind of the spirit person and the mind of the living person; and my spirit guides will only come forward when I invite them, give them formal permission to do so.

When I am about to enter a trance, I like to sit on a comfortable chair in a dimly-lit, preferably candle-lit, room where the telephones have been unplugged and where I am unlikely to be interrupted or disturbed. I begin by closing my eyes and focusing on my breathing, letting my attention rest on the ingoing and outgoing breaths. I do this for a few minutes until my body and mind become quieter and calmer and I am fully relaxed. Then, silently within my own mind, I address the spirits saying: 'Welcome friends. If you are able to come close, that would be wonderful for the people who are gathered here with me right now.'

At some point, I then add in a very respectful formal way: 'Zintar, I now give you permission to come forward and blend your mind with my mind, so that all who are gathered here may hear your voice when you speak through me.'

I have never really fathomed out what follows this entreaty, but the moment I give Zintar permission to come forward, it is as if I begin to slip to one side of my body and mind and enter a realm that is so warm, relaxed and delightful that it is almost like being wrapped in a soft duvet. Moments later I feel Zintar move closer to me and I am told that my body begins to take on the appearance of an ancient Tibetan. This transfiguration is invariably followed by the need for me to clear my throat as he prepares to talk through me.

When he begins to speak, I seem to settle back into my mind and listen to the conversation that ensues. Sometimes, when the trance is only a light one, I hear every word that he says; at other times, when the trance is a deep one, I cannot recall anything that has been said.

Trance really is one of the most fascinating aspects of mediumship; and, over the years, I have found that the more I engage in it, the stronger and deeper the trances become. I love enabling spirits to come close and say what *they* want to say, without my mind getting in the way or consciously putting its own interpretation on what is being said.

Sometimes it is Zintar who comes to speak, sometimes Star. When Zintar comes he is happy to offer philosophy, or words of wisdom, or perhaps talk about life in the spirit world. Star's approach, however, is very different. He is often light-hearted and, on one-to-one trance occasions, always requires the person who is present with me to sit facing me and hold my hands.

As soon as their fingers touch my hand, I feel as if I am travelling back through time and space; and, sometimes, when I come out of the trance, I learn that, although I have little or no recall of what has happened or been said, Star has actually been speaking directly to the person or people who are with me about their life or their loved ones in the spirit world. They may also have transfigured the features of one of their loved ones over my face. Transfiguration moments are *very* special and absolutely breathtaking for the people concerned.

At other times Star talks to them about their soul 'mission' and the 'path' they need to take in order to overcome various trials and tribulations and fulfil the purpose of this particular lifetime.

One occasion I recall vividly was when Star, having asked a lady to sit facing me and hold my hands, then said: 'I can tell from your energy levels that you have been feeling very poorly of late, not at all well.'

When the lady confirmed that she had been suffering from a cancerous condition for a year or so, but was now in remission, Star let go of her hands, placed his hands on her shoulders and began a healing session.

When the session was over, the lady said it was the most extraordinary experience she had ever had in her entire life.

'When he placed his hands on my shoulders,' she said, 'it was as if an electric current had entered my body and, seconds later, I experienced intense heat on one shoulder and intense cold on the other. Although I had my eyes closed, I was aware of being immersed in a turquoise colour and, as I relaxed more and more into what felt like the gentle flow of a warm turquoise liquid, I felt myself imbued with a sense of healing and well-being.

'After a few moments when I opened my eyes,' she added, 'I saw a man's face transfigured over your face. It was the face of a very ancient man, with Mongolian-like features, yet his skin was soft, smooth and totally unlined. At one moment as I sat there looking at him, his eyes opened even though I could see that beneath his eyes, your eyes were closed. Then, as he looked directly into my eyes, I felt this incredible sense of being healed and made whole again. I can't actually recall many of the words he said,' she continued, 'because the overwhelming sense was that of being touched by the spirit world.

'The next day,' she continued, 'I woke up feeling *so* well, *so* full of zest and energy it was just as if I was nineteen years old again. All in all,' she added, 'that experience of trance is something I shall never forget, something that I will treasure for the rest of my life.'

During a recent trance session, which I conducted in the presence of five of my friends, Stuart, Vicky, Mandy, Diane and David, they decided to begin by asking Zintar some questions.

'It would be *really* nice if you were to tell us something about yourself and your work with Tony, your medium,' Stuart began.

The answer channelled through me while I was in a deep trance was as follows: 'My dearest wish is to do my best to help and inspire people who come to mediums hoping for a glimpse of the unseen world beyond the earthly world in which they are now living. My most fervent hope is that such seekers, who have taken the trouble to give up some of their time from the usual business of earthly life, will be blessed by being able to hear the eternal truth that there is no such thing as death; that there is a continuum of *life* within your world, the world of the living, and life within our world, the world of spirits.

'As for Tony, he and I have always been friends who remain connected with each other after death and throughout each of his various incarnations. Sometimes our roles are reversed and we play different parts within the theatre of life. At other times I simply find the best way I can to bring all the wisdom I have gained throughout my many lives to enrich and guide him in his work for others.'

When it was Vicky's turn to put her question, she said: 'Why are we here on earth? And is it true that we are destined to live through one reincarnation after another?'

'Whether or not we choose to be reincarnated and to return to earth is up to us as individuals,' Zintar replied. 'But reincarnation should be regarded as a blessing that gives individual spirits endless opportunities to resolve what lies behind the trials and tribulations they have experienced in the past and, in so doing, achieve a greater understanding of themselves and of others.

'The law of karma, which is relevant to all our births, is really quite simple: What goes around, comes around! The choice is ours. We sow and reap the seeds of our actions; and the harvest may be to our greater or lesser good. Human life, with all its passions and complexities can dull our vision and baffle the mind, and fear of the unknown can render a person impotent. The seeker of truth must always try to lead a balanced life by keeping to the middle path and avoiding too many conflicting distractions, desires and excesses. If, in addition the concept of "Love thy neighbour" is always held in mind, good will prevail; and, one day, union with God, the Great Spirit, will enable us to live in a permanent state of peace, harmony and bliss.

'Each of you, who are present here today, has elected to serve others and you have already learned that, in order to do this to the best of your ability, you must make the most of every opportunity and challenge that is presented to you. Then, as each incarnation comes to a natural end, you will be able to leave the earth better equipped emotionally, mentally and spiritually than when you arrived. Then, having "rested" a while, you can decide whether to return to earth for more!'

'You spoke of God earlier,' Mandy said. 'Is God one great spirit and entity, or a collective of spirits and entities?'

'There is more to God than the human mind can ever fully comprehend. We are speaking of an all-embracing, all-powerful, all creative celestial force that permeates and irradiates the whole universe with love. Yet each of us is a spark of that eternal celestial flame and each of us has the potential to blend with and merge with that universal power for the good.

'Over the period of many lives, those who seek the truth learn how to detach themselves from earthly passions and desires, from things material, and they gladly give up their small self, their egocentric ways, in order to blend with God, the greater Self, who is beyond self-ishness and self-interest, and who loves and cares for each of us – the good, the bad and the indifferent – in equal measure.'

After a moment when the group had spent a little time absorbing what Zintar had just said, David said: 'You spoke earlier of the spirit world. Could you, please, tell us what you know about that domain?'

'The spirit world is vast and, as there is still much that I have to learn and discover, I can only speak of what I know. Within my world, which is a realm of incomparable beauty, there is endless sunshine that shines down upon us from the top of mountain peaks and then descends to dazzle the world below. Here, I live in peace and harmony within a brotherhood of spirits who, like myself, have dedicated their lives to helping and guiding others – much in the way that I am doing at this moment. Here, in a place where love rules supreme and "the lion lies down with the lamb", no harm befalls anybody and we are infused with a healing warmth and all the colours of the rainbow. It is a place to come home to, a place of rest where the light is brighter than any light you have ever seen, and the colours more vivid than any colour the human mind could imagine. It is a place where one's spirit is lovingly laid bare, so that we can see all that has been and all that we still have the potential to be. Having seen what we need to see, we are able to embark upon the next stage of a journey that, given the right influences and choices made, will bring us ever closer to self-realisation and to God.'

'Please can you explain what we experience when passing over?' Stuart then asked.

'Death is there to draw you like a magnet from the life that you have just lived to the world of spirit,' Zintar explained. 'And we spirits await you just beyond the circle of light that you see at the end of the tunnel. "*Come back to us, come*," we call to you in soft welcoming voices that are full of love, compassion and reassurance. Some people who arrive here have no belief in the afterlife and, convinced that they are dead, they choose to sleep a while. Sooner or later, however, they realise that death is an illusion and they are helped to accept what lies in store for them. Others may also sleep for a short while; then, having received a warm welcome from the spirits, they begin to enjoy being reunited with loved ones who are already in the spirit world, and are happy to await the day when they will be reunited once again with the loved ones they have left behind them on earth.

'It can, of course, take time for a person to adjust. The actual passing over is easier for those who do not have very strong bonds with anybody left behind on earth. For mothers who find themselves separated from their children, or husbands who are missing their wives, and so on and so forth, the transition can take longer. But that phase will pass as they become aware that death is only a temporary pause, and that they will be reunited one day in the afterlife and will also spend more time together on earth.'

'There is a lot of talk about children coming back into our world with the kind of knowledge that it has taken us between twenty and thirty years to acquire,' Vicky was then inspired to say. 'Is this all part of a master plan to make the world more spiritually aware?'

'What you are speaking of here are enlightened beings who have become highly evolved spiritually and wish to use the knowledge and wisdom they have acquired for the welfare of others and the world. Having chosen to be reincarnated, they return to earth with the hope of inspiring others to lead more spiritually based lives. To help them in this work, they often grow up to become teachers, philosophers, healers, ambassadors and leaders.

'Such beings, who choose to return to earth in order to dedicate their lives to others, do shine more brightly from a very early age; and, collectively, they form a powerhouse for good in a troubled world and they are there for those who have already evolved to a stage where they are blessed with ears that hear and eyes that see.'

'We are surrounded by friends and family on earth,' Mandy then said, 'who we have been told were part of our life's journey before. Do you have any thoughts on this?'

'Yes, it is love that draws us all together and you may well have shared many lives with the same people and may continue to do so in the future. Sometimes when you meet someone for the first time, there is instant recognition and, after a few minutes, you feel as if you have known that person all your life, and you are convinced that you have met before. These people are part of what is called your soul group, and you may well have fulfilled different roles in each other's lives during previous incarnations. Whether you were once mother to the child you are now cradling in your arms, or the child was once mother to you, will remain a mystery. The only thing that matters ultimately is the love that is given and received and shared, and what impact that has in helping us to achieve our full potential and evolve spiritually.'

'We have been truly blessed by your presence today,' Diane said. 'Do you have any messages to pass on to us?'

'Always remember that there is strength in numbers and that it is good for like-minded people, who desire to increase their knowledge of the truth, to seek each other out and spend time together. With very rare exceptions, we always risk falling by the wayside when we set off alone, so always ensure that the pathway between you remains open. Working for the welfare of others can be very demanding, and you will achieve far more when you combine your various talents and work collectively as a group. So my message to you today is: continue to trust and to love one another, so that you may be better equipped to continue to evolve as a powerhouse for the good in the universe.'

During the actual trance, which was a very deep one on this occasion, I was completely unaware of the questions that were being asked and of Zintar's replies. This meant that I was even more delighted that Stuart had recorded the session, so that I could share in what I would otherwise have missed! To hear Zintar's voice vibrating through my vocal chords is always a thrill and I have always felt very blessed to have him in my life as my spirit guide. Each time we come together, my desire to become a better instrument for his use increases ten-fold.

'Come again soon,' I say, silently, as if speaking to one of my oldest and dearest friends. But, then, in reality, that's exactly what I am doing!

Some years ago, Stuart and I and two of our friends, Carol and Gwen, travelled to Cardiff to attend a physical mediumship seminar. It was an action-packed, exciting weekend and, on the way home when I was driving, Stuart was in the passenger seat fast asleep and the two girls had also drifted off in the back of the car.

At one point in the long monotonous journey along the busy motorway, I looked away from the road ahead to check the direction signs.

The next thing I knew was the sound of Stuart's voice screaming: 'T–O–N–Y!'

And, as I jumped out of my skin and looked back at the road, all I could see was a blaze of red brake and hazard lights flashing ahead of me. The car in front, which was now only about twenty feet from our car, had stalled and was stationary.

As I slammed on the brakes and, simultaneously, wrenched the steering wheel to the left, the car tilted to one side and skidded off the road on to the hard shoulder, followed by at least half-a-dozen cars that were behind us.

Sitting there, trying to get my breath back, I realised that we had just had a *very* close shave with death – so close, it was a miracle we had avoided a life-threatening crash.

As soon as my passengers had righted themselves and regained their composure, I said: 'I'm *SO* sorry. I was looking out for a slip road and didn't realise the car in front had stopped. Thank God for Stuart's sharp eyes.'

'Don't thank me!' Stuart exclaimed. 'I was fast asleep when I heard a spirit voice booming in my ear: "*Wake up. Look out*! *Wake up*!" And, when I did, with barely a second to spare, I saw a sea of red lights ahead of us.'

'I wonder why the spirits didn't warn me?' I said.

But the answer was obvious. I was *so* engrossed in reading the road signs, I might not have heard them even if they had tried. So, they did the next best thing. They alerted Stuart who was then able to save us from injury or death.

I certainly believe that the spirits were looking after us on that road from Cardiff and that we owed our lives to them that night.

* * *

During the twenty years that I have been interested in the paranormal, I have always had an intense fascination with what is known as electronic voice phenomena (EVP). The very thought that spirits can leave audible messages for all to hear on a tape recorder or television, whether the person has a mediumistic gift or not, excites me beyond belief and sends shivers up my spine. I have never ceased to think that it is totally amazing that our departed loved ones can come and go and confirm they are still around and very much part of our lives.

For anyone who has not come across EVP it will probably sound too good to be true, but I can assure you that it works. All that is needed is a tape recorder, a blank tape and a lot of patience. The way it works is simple enough to explain, but not so simple I assume for the spirit people to achieve. It is important to invite them into the experiment, explaining either out loud or silently in your mind, what you wish to happen. Then, having set the play and record function on the tape recorder, the spirit people will hopefully endeavour to project their voices on to the tape itself.

How they do this I do not know, I just know they can.

Many's the time when, after just a few minutes of recording, I have played the tape back, listened intently and been rewarded with a whisper or a loud clear spirit voice saying 'hello' or 'can you hear me?'

Now, for some people, this may not seem much to get so worked up about, but for those of us who are privileged to hear such a voice, a voice that is often filled with emotion, it is yet another confirmation that those who have gone before us can indeed make contact.

Over the years I have been fortunate enough to have taken part in some very successful experiments in EVP, and I have heard many names, sentences, words of encouragement and messages of love called out from beyond the grave. Whether these are left as whispers on a tape recorder, or as images on a flickering TV screen, EVP leaves even hardened sceptics dumbfounded.

Late in 2004, for example, I met Jane Fryer, a reporter for the *Daily Express* and, after our meeting, she produced the following article about one of the EVP experiments I was privileged to be a part of. Jane has kindly allowed me to reproduce her article here in my book.

The group huddled around a small low table in a dusty room, tense and quiet as a tape spooled in the battered black recorder before them. But, as Tony Stockwell pressed stop, rewind and then play, the silence of the past ten minutes was gone. Clearly audible, over and over, louder and louder, was the word 'Julie'. Pauline Flanders promptly burst into tears.

'It's my daughter, Julie, who died as a toddler, twenty-five years ago. That was the voice we used to hear,' she said.

Ten minutes earlier the mood had been lighter. Pauline, fifty, and from Liverpool, had been teased after telling how, in the eighties, she had heard spirit voices on her second child's baby monitor. 'It was probably the local cab firm,' one of the group had laughed, but the recording came as a shock to them.

Essex psychic medium Stockwell is no stranger to unexplained voices, however. He is a collector of 'electronic voice phenomena'. Commonly known as EVP, these are mysterious voices or voice-like sounds, often distorted, that can crop up on radios, tape recordings, answering machines or in TV pictures. EVP has been given the Hollywood treatment and will have a much higher, considerably scarier, profile after *White Noise*, a film starring Michael Keaton, is released. Keaton plays an architect who becomes obsessed with EVP after his murdered wife contacts him from beyond the grave. For Stockwell, however, there is nothing scary about EVP. He claims it is simply a 'wonderful way of communicating with the other side'. He is not alone. Today more than 50,000 people around the world spend their time taping voices beyond the grave using ordinary cassette recorders. Even the Vatican has taken an interest, disregarding Leviticus' warnings about summoning spirits to discover whether the recordings can prove there's an afterlife.

The key to EVP is that, while voices appear on the recorded version, they are not audible when the recording is being made. 'It's only when you play back the tape that suddenly you hear this independent voice,' says Stockwell. 'There's something strange about the quality of it – as if it is the spirit person projecting the memory of their voice on to the tape.'

One EVP instance I am now recalling was when I was doing a one-to-one reading for a gentleman, named Fred. About a minute into the reading, I realised that the tape recorder had switched itself off and was not recording.

'Excuse me,' I said. 'I'll just rewind the tape and we will start again.'

But as I leaned over to press the rewind button, I absent-mindedly pressed the 'play' button by mistake. As I did so, I suddenly heard a faint voice saying something on the tape: 'Did you hear that?' I asked him.

'Yes, I did,' he replied.

'Well it *wasn't* our voices,' I added. 'So it must be an EVP voice.'

Then, as we both paused and listened, we heard the voice more clearly this time repeating the name: 'Montgomery', followed a short while later by: 'Montgomery Place'.

As Fred said this name didn't ring any bells for him, however, I just took a few moments to explain EVP and continued with the reading.

A couple of days later, just as I was about to leave my house, I received a phone call from Fred, who sounded very excited: 'Do you remember,' he said, 'that during my reading you talked a great deal about my maternal grandmother and gave me some very accurate details about her personality, what she looked like, and how she passed.'

'Yes,' I said. 'I do remember.'

'Well,' he replied. 'I have something quite extraordinary to report back to you. Last night when I was telling my mother all about our meeting I mentioned the disembodied voice on the tape recorder repeating the name Montgomery Place and she became very agitated and interrupted me. "Did you say *Montgomery Place*?" she asked me, shocked. "Yes," I replied. "Well, I'll be . . ." she exclaimed. "You won't recall this, but your maternal grandmother lived in *Montgomery Place* for many years and *that*, son, was where *I* was born."'

After Fred and I had said our fond goodbyes again, I stood there for a moment smiling. Then, raising my eyes to the spirits, I said: 'You know what? You *never* cease to surprise me and the people I'm reading for, and I'm *so* glad you don't.'

Another spiritual surprise I remember was when I was in my early twenties, a time when I used to do a lot of spiritual healing. During these sessions, I would lay my hands on people and pray that, with the help of the spirit world, they would be healed in mind, body and spirit.

On one particular occasion, when I was working in a

candle-lit room in a church on Canvey Island, there were only about half-a-dozen people present, and we put on some lovely soothing music while I was healing an elderly lady, called Doris, who had very painful arthritic joints. I had been healing Doris for several weeks and each time she came, she told me she was feeling a little bit better and certainly more cheerful.

On this occasion when I was healing her, I placed my hands as usual over the top of her head, but I felt them being guided by the spirits to come to rest just a couple of inches from her face. As they did so, I became aware that Doris was becoming very excited and tearful.

Withdrawing my hands, I said: 'Are you okay, Doris?'

'Oh, yes! *Please* don't stop,' she replied through her tears. '*Please* put your hands back over my face.'

As I did as she requested, she became quiet, but remained tearful.

When the healing session came to an end, she said: 'That was absolutely *wonderful*!'

'*Why*? What happened?' I asked mystified.

'Well, when you put your hands over my face,' she replied. 'I immediately became aware of the smell of Blue Grass, the perfume my dear old mum always used, and the fragrance was so strong I thought for one moment that somebody present in the room must be wearing it. But, then, there was more! Having been reminded of my mum, I started to think about my dad and the next moment there was such a strong smell of the tobacco he used to smoke in his pipe that I thought he was standing next to me. This was then followed by such a strong image of my mum and dad together in the spirit world that I began to wonder if my dear husband, Tom, was also with them. Then, as your hands hovered over my face, I started to smell Old Spice, the aftershave that Tom always used; and this was followed by a wonderful vision of all three of them standing together.'

Doris was clearly thrilled that she had experienced so much during the healing session; and her arthritis, she told me later, had never felt better than it did right then!

This connection with loved ones through the sense of smell was a common occurrence that year. Practically every time I placed my hands close to somebody's face during healing sessions, they commented afterwards that they had smelled one thing or another that had a strong association with different people in their lives.

I did wonder for a while if their imagination was running wild and they were jumping on to each other's bandwagons. But then something happened that convinced me otherwise! As I drew my hands away after these healing sessions, I noticed that they smelled very sweet, just as if somebody had rubbed them all over with almond oil. Then, on closer inspection, I noticed a slight oily film stretching across the palms of my hand and when I rubbed them together the smell would change to another smell and then another until there was a whole symphony of different smells. On one occasion, I decided to play with the spirits and, having rubbed my hands together, I said aloud, 'Wouldn't it be lovely if you started to smell of old leather' and a moment later they did!

I can only surmise from all this that there were spirits around at that time who enjoyed experimenting with the use of certain phenomena and, during this particular period, it was nostalgic smells!

Another truly amazing way that the spirit world is able to indulge in comings and goings, and make contact, is via automatic writing. When I am engaging the spirits in this way I simply hold a pen in my hand and position it in such a way that the nib sits quite tightly on a sheet of paper. I then ask the spirit people to write down anything, in words, that he or she would like to express. A moment or so later I get the feeling that my hand and my arm no longer belong to me. It is just as if they are being guided by an unseen force. At this point I usually glance away and focus on something in the room or the garden. This neutralises any thoughts that may influence or interfere with the proceedings. After a few moments, I feel the pen start to move in my hand and words begin to form themselves on the paper.

What is interesting is that these words appear in very different styles of handwriting, and the form of expression is also very different. Likewise, on very rare occasions, they appear in a foreign language. Personally, I have no doubt that the words emanate from the spirit world.

It would be possible, of course, for a medium's subconscious to play a part in the proceedings, but if we remain true to the spirits and evoke their minds to take control there is no way we could be considered responsible for the kind of intimate information that comes through. 'The proof,' people are fond of saying, 'is in the pudding' and this is the case with automatic writing when the information that is given is so detailed and so personal that we could not have simply dreamed it up.

One rather sad disturbing experience I recall that concerned automatic writing occurred not so very long ago. Having sat there for some time with the pen poised, a lady's first and second name appeared on the paper, and was subsequently followed by the message: *They put me down so deep, nobody will ever find me, but I am happy now.*

When I checked out the name on the Internet, I discovered that, lo and behold, it was exactly as the spirit had described. The name belonged to a missing person and, as no knowledge of her whereabouts had ever been established, her fate had remained unknown.

There was no way that I could have known that name without the automatic writing experience, but, once it had occurred, I knew that the missing person was no longer with us and that, although her human remains would never be found, she had at least made it clear that she was happy now in the other world.

I can only add, as with so many things to do with the paranormal, it is not possible to say with certainty why some spirits choose EVP or automatic writing as their method of communication. But why not? If they are there, hoping to make contact, or in a playful mood, and a machine happens to be running or a medium is conveniently holding a pen or pencil, I can well understand that they might well seize the moment!

Why, for example, do our spirit guides choose to watch over us and do their utmost to keep us from harm? Certainly, whether we are aware of it or not, I believe that each of us is granted one of these heavenly beings; and that, from the moment we are born, our guide takes up residence by our side to shield us from harm and offer us guidance when it is needed. Whether or not we recognise or acknowledge their presence and influence on our life, I am sure that *they* remain constant in their desire to reach out and comfort us during troubled times.

Many people, including those who have never visited a psychic or a medium, or been inside a Spiritualist church, share my belief in guardian angels – angelic souls in the higher realms – spirit guides, enlightened beings, who exist to bring support and comfort to their earthly charges whenever they are in need.

Such beings are also particularly aware when somebody is

dying or crossing over, and they endeavour to bring them to an understanding of what is happening to them. After all, some of the new arrivals may not have had any belief in the afterlife when they were alive; and some who may have passed in a tragically sudden way do not have time to prepare their mind for what is going on, or for what is in store for them.

As a medium, though, I can only offer my belief that when we pass on, those who love us and have gone before are there to meet and welcome us. They take us under their wing, envelop us in their love, and help to soothe and heal our troubled minds.

This is what happens, I believe, whether it is an individual person who has just passed or countless people. And when those who are left to mourn and grieve, and cry out in deep anguish after such outrages: 'Where was God when this happened?' I can only reply gently, but with utter conviction: 'He was *there* – giving comfort to each and every person in their hour of need.'

That sense I have of an ever-present omnipresence reminds me of some lines by Kahlil Gibran.

The mist that drifts away at dawn, leaving but dew in the field, shall rise and gather into a cloud and then fall down in rain.

And not unlike the mist have I been.

In the stillness of the night I have walked in your streets, and my spirit has entered your houses,

And your heartbeats were in my heart, and your breath was upon my face, and I knew you all.

Ay, I knew your joy and your pain, and in your sleep your dreams were my dreams.

And oftentimes I was among you a lake among the mountains.

I mirrored the summits in you and the bending slopes,
and even the passing flocks of your thoughts and your
desires.

What beautiful lines those are – and what more could we ask
of the Great Spirit, that He should be there, that every hair on
our head should be counted, and that not even a sparrow
should fall from the sky without His knowledge.

Whether we have been brought up in a religious household
or not, we have all heard, usually from infancy onwards,
about God; and most of us at one time or another have been
told to say our prayers or, as adults, have lifted our eyes to
heaven and asked for help and guidance.

This belief that there is something or someone out there in
the great beyond, who can help and guide us, is a fundamental
belief that so many of us share. Exactly what this God – or
ultimate power – *is*, remains for the majority of us something
of a mystery.

In my day-to-day work I meet a lot of people who tell me
they believe in an afterlife, yet they are not comfortable about
saying they believe in God. When, however, I ask them if they
believe in a universal creative force, a love that can conquer all,
they admit they do; and when I then begin to discuss God in
this way, describing Him/Her as a powerful force for good, a
loving energy that connects all things together, most people
seem to agree *that* is what they believe in, too.

In addition to God, I believe there are universal messengers,
leaders and healers, who have never lived a physical life here
on earth; and these beings, who are pure and untouched by the
problems and temptations of this world, have been throughout the ages referred to as angels. Frequently seen and described by seers and visionaries, they appear within the
writings of many of the world's major religions and have

often been attributed with acts of great kindness and being at the scenes of many of the world's major disasters.

Imagine how it must be for angels, who so desire all things good, true and beautiful for us, to witness man's madness and the wars of the world. It is my belief that, having tried so hard to influence the minds of those who perpetrate such terrible acts, they must weep a thousand tears.

In turbulent troubled times I also believe that angels do everything in their power to help us to be strong and to stand firm whenever we encounter things that are unjust or harmful to ourselves or others. I believe it is they who give us the strength to stand up and be counted, and to take responsibility and help create change for the good within our societies. Each of us has God within us, each of us has the ability to be touched by angelic forces; and each of us has the power to help combat dark forces within our midst.

Things on earth go wrong when people cease to be in tune with their own true identity, when they lose themselves in materialism, or seek self-glorification and no longer listen to that inner voice that tries to penetrate their thoughts in their waking and sleeping hours. *That* voice is the voice of their own soul, their own spirit, the part of them that is intrinsically connected to the whole – and the ultimate creative power. When man is governed by desire and self-interest alone, things go very wrong indeed. Angels, however, have the ability to inspire the living and evoke an energy so powerful that real change can occur. With their help amazing miraculous things can happen.

Some years ago when I was working in Germany offering readings and giving demonstrations, I was invited out to dinner at a local restaurant to meet a number of like-minded people. Just as we finished eating I became aware of an elderly lady sitting at the end of our table, who was looking at me with such an earnest fixed gaze that I felt rather unnerved for a moment. When I smiled at her, however, she beckoned me to come and sit beside her.

Having introduced herself as Marta, she took my hand in hers and began to recount an experience she had had many years before.

'When I was a child,' she told me, 'I was always rather sickly and, for most of my childhood, I was denied the pleasure of playing outside with other children.'

Her parents, she continued, lived in a large house in Hamburg and, realising she was intensely lonely, they invited a neighbour's child to visit her often. In no time at all, the two girls, who enjoyed playing together, became great friends. One day, feeling mischievous, they decided it would be fun to play sliding down the banisters, something they had been expressly forbidden to do. The staircase in the house was huge and when looked down upon, from the top to the bottom, seemed to go on forever. Unperturbed, however, Marta placed one leg over the banister, then, having pushed off, let herself go and began the rapid descent. For a while all was well, but then one of her petticoats got caught on the deeply carved wooden spindles.

'I can remember hearing a ripping sound and feeling scared, then jerked to a sudden halt I lost my grip,' she told me.

She remembered slipping sideways from the bannister into the stairwell and, as she did so, crying out: *'Please, God, help me, don't let me die.'* Then, as though time stood still, she found herself suspended.

'I was held in mid-air by a brilliant white light,' she said. 'And I no longer felt afraid. On the contrary, I felt calm and peaceful. Then I heard a lady's voice.'

The voice, she said, spoke to her in a soothing tone, but she was left with no recollection of what she had heard.

'The light just wrapped itself around me like a soft blanket,' she said. 'Then, having done that, it lowered me gently down on to the floor below.'

Later that night, when I was reflecting on what Marta had told me, I had an immediate inkling of what had happened. There are times when angels are able to penetrate the earth's atmosphere in order to help us here below. Why they helped, Marta, though, when so many children perish and are not saved, I cannot explain. I truly do not have the answer. What I do know is that God and his host of helpers – the angels – *can and do* work miracles.

I know I am fond of saying I am blessed, but that's how I feel. Perhaps, in part, this is because I am not only blessed with an awareness of the guardian angels, I am also blessed with my spirit guides, Zintar and Star, who always seem to be there just when I need them most. So, *doubly* blessed – and *doubly* grateful – am I! And, as if that were not sufficient riches for one lifetime, I found myself *trebly* blessed when one day I received one of those telephone calls that come out of the blue – a telephone call that included the following question: How would you like to try something different for a new TV series? How would you like to be taken to unknown destinations in a foreign country where you will be asked to unlock the answers to mysterious events that happened somewhere back in time?

How could I resist!

'Okay,' I said to the guy from IPM, a television company I had worked for before. 'That sounds just fine to me.'

After all, as somebody who believes there is nothing to fear but fear itself, there was no other answer worthy of my consideration.

My brief for the first episode, I then discovered, was to pack for all weathers, make sure I did not leave my passport behind and turn up at Stansted Airport at a certain time! That was all I was told.

So, some time later, I found myself at Stansted waiting to collect my ticket to an undisclosed top-secret destination, wondering what on earth I had let myself in for. All sorts of thoughts, alongside images of exotic places, were cascading through my mind. Would the plane touch down in Hawaii, Barbados, Bermuda, the Seychelles?

I am constantly amazed by how many different ways a psychic can work. Feeling and sensing the energies around a person or place is, of course, an everyday event, the norm for many of us. But being asked to pick up, receive, information from a place that is hundreds or even thousands of years old is *not* the norm – and I found the thought of that very exciting. In the event, working in this way proved to be rather like peeling an onion, taking away one layer after another of the history of a building until one reached the kernel – and it was a truly fascinating way to work.

There was an interesting encounter at the start of this first episode of the series. During an informal chat, the young lady, who was the assistant producer, made it abundantly clear to me that, as far as she was concerned, the kind of work I did was a lot of nonsense.

'I *don't* believe in any kind of afterlife,' she stated. 'As far as I am concerned when you are dead, you are *dead* and *that's that*.'

When I did not rise to the bait and go on the defensive, she added more gently: 'I'm sure you are *very* sincere and that you believe in what you do, but I honestly cannot go along with any of it.'

What she didn't know was that while she was speaking, I was aware of a man's presence at my side and I could hear the name that he was mentioning loud and clear. Looking the assistant producer straight in the eye, I said: 'Do you know a man called John?'

Her response was one of shock, then horror.

'Do you know a man called John,' I repeated. 'Because this man is very insistent and is telling me that he passed very recently to the other world and he wants to send his love to you and your mum.'

The moment I finished speaking, she burst into tears and fled from the room.

When she sought me out later in the day, she said: 'I must admit I am *baffled*. Nobody here knows my father died recently and nobody knows his name was John, so there's no way you could just have picked that up.'

I was *so* pleased for her. She had been so sure, so adamant about what she believed and now, confronted by something that she could not explain, it was clear that she was having to reconsider and reassess all her former beliefs.

The team working for this particular programme, which was entitled the *Legend Detectives*, was made up of the presenter, Ronald, an historian called Tessa, a psychologist called Massimo and a psychic – me.

And one of the locations proved to be Naples. I had never been there or to any other part of Italy before and I was bowled over by *napoletanità*, a truly heady mix of heart-stopping mayhem and life being lived to its chaotic limit. I found it almost overwhelming. I had never seen so many people careering around on scooters and motorbikes without crash-helmets, and every car seemed to be full of bumps, chips, scratches and dents. Some looked like write-offs with only their engines still intact!

On the first day of filming, while I was still recovering from all these new impressions, I was driven to a very arid desolate place that reeked of sulphurous springs. Once there, I was asked to let my mind travel back in time to AD 305 and then tell the team what I sensed – saw and felt. It was a bit of a tall order because the place was absolutely bursting its seams with layer after layer of history – and every emotion known to man was present, vibrating there.

'The first thing I'd like to say,' I murmured, 'is that this place was *not* always the arid desolate place it is today. Once upon a time it was a beautiful oasis, with lovely marble fountains, and a magnificent white temple standing just there.'

Ronald, the presenter, later confirmed that it had once been an oasis – and a very popular Roman spa.

Looking at Ronald, I then described a vision I had just seen – a vision of a man dressed in a long, flowing toga-like robe, who had just made it clear to me that he had been tortured in this place for refusing to denounce Christianity and do a pagan leader's bidding. He had then been dragged off and beheaded.

'This is *very* bizarre,' I commented to the presenter. 'But, as the poor man lay bleeding to death, blood was taken from him and placed into some kind of vessel.'

Again, it was confirmed that local legend had always had it that as the man lay dying, an old man gathered up his body and severed head, and placed them reverently in a cloth. Meanwhile, a Neapolitan woman soaked up the spilled blood with a sponge and filled a phial with the precious red liquid. I was then told his name was San Gennaro, previously Saint Januarius, Bishop of Benevento, before he became revered by the Neapolitans as their protector and martyr and adopted as the patron saint of Naples. The blood that was taken at the time of his beheading is still preserved in two glass balsamaries and stored in the treasury of the Cathedral Church of Naples. At frequent intervals, apparently, during the past seventeen hundred years, the brown, powdery substance is said to have miraculously liquefied and transformed itself into the familiar red blood of a living being.

The next day, while I was still absorbing all this, I was taken to the Catacomb Di S. Gennaro. Having descended the steps into the catacomb, which has a higher and a lower level, I could see that the entire place was stacked, from floor to ceiling, with hundreds of differing-size burial chambers, including some tiny ones for babies.

Later on when I was reading through a tourist pamphlet, I discovered that San Gennaro had first become a very special and adored saint for the Neapolitans after he protected them, and Naples, from a cataclysmic eruption of the nearby Mount Vesuvius. Apparently when the volcano erupted, all the villagers had fled and taken refuge in the church, and prayed fervently to San Gennaro.

'*Please spare our lives, please save us,*' they implored – and he did!

The terrifying flow of red-hot lava, which devoured and burned everything to white ashes in its path, stopped just short of the church itself, saving the lives of all those who had taken shelter within its walls. And, to this day, San Gennaro's devotees believe that their patron saint's powers of protection transcended death and that he continues to protect them and their city from harm. In fact, in every emergency, San Gennaro is the Neapolitans' all-powerful champion and universal helper for all kinds of threats and troubles.

During my time in Naples, I also picked up on something that, for me, was even stronger and more important than anything I had gleaned about the legend of San Gennaro.

Between filming various shots, when I had time to wander around on my own, I was constantly aware in my mind of the sound of a woman screaming and crying out to me. Needless to say, the manifestation of such a persistent sound, within the cool, dark, sinister catacombs, a place that was full of subtle vibrations and memories, was *very* disturbing.

As I continued to wander down one of the catacombs, the sound still resounding within my inner ear, I came to an archway where there were some more steps descending to a small chamber-like room, a cell within a cell. As I descended the steps, the scream and cries suddenly ceased and, in their place, I heard a woman's voice saying, '*You're here – let me show you what happened to me . . .*'

Then, as I came to a halt within the chamber, I had an immediate vision of a slim, beautiful, young woman, with long, raven-black hair, who was dressed in a white tunic like those worn in Roman times.

The immediate impression I had was that she had been a seer, a young mystic, who had had the power of healing in her hands. A much sought after person in the community, she was constantly asked to attend births and preside at the bedsides of ill and dying dignitaries. Inevitably, perhaps, she had got on the wrong side of some local priests, who frowned upon women playing such a prominent role in their community, and they had taken it upon themselves to show her the error of her ways.

One day when she was invited to join four priests in the lower reaches of the catacomb where I was now standing, she, in all innocence, had thought that she was going to join them in a ceremony to do with the death of a nobleman.

She was sadly misguided in this belief and it proved to be a fatal mistake.

Having got her there, the treatment that the priests had then meted out to her, 'for her greater good', had included certain physical abuses 'to oust the devil from her' and this torture had eventually resulted in her death.

Thought to be dead but, in reality, still clinging to life, she had been placed in one of the catacomb's burial cavities, which had then been bricked up – and there she had been left to breathe her last breath.

As soon as I heard all that she wanted to tell me, the vision of her dissolved and I heard no more screaming.

'What an horrendous fate for somebody who had obviously done so much good work in her community,' I thought. 'How terrible to be so misunderstood by the priesthood and persecuted and tortured because a) she was a woman, b) the priests obviously found her threatening and c) because she was so well known, so sought after and so loved by the people she helped.'

As these thoughts drifted out of my mind, the young spirit came through again and made it clear to me that, having made the initial contact, she was no longer interested in dwelling on the past and she just kept repeating: '*Now you will know me.*'

'But *how* will I know you?' I asked mystified. 'And what is your name? *Please* tell me your name.'

'My name is *not* important – I am a spirit,' she replied, simply.

'But your name *is* important to me,' I pleaded.

Almost instantaneously, I then heard her say: 'All right. You may know me as Veronica.'

Although I sensed that this was *not* her name when she was alive, but just a name she had chosen to pacify me, I replied: 'It's so nice to meet you, Veronica.'

The next moment the vision faded again and, although I tried to call her back, I heard no more.

Later that same day, when we were doing some more filming, this time in a graffiti-ridden, run-down area of Naples, I became aware of a little girl, aged about seven, peering out from between some lines of washing that was hanging out to dry. A real street urchin, with grubby face and hands and wearing a faded, frayed-at-the-hem cotton dress, I immediately noticed that she had the same striking raven-black hair that I had seen earlier.

Then, clear as day, amidst all the chaos of motorbikes and scooters roaring past, I saw a vision of Veronica, dressed in the same long white robes, manifest alongside the child. That was surprising enough, but more surprising still the little girl suddenly crossed over to me and, tugging at my sleeve, she looked me straight in the eye, and whispered urgently: '*You see her, too. You see her, too.*'

'Yes, I do,' I replied astonished, but before I could say another word she gave me a beatific smile and walked away. The next moment she had disappeared into a narrow alleyway that ran between the dilapidated houses. As she did so, the vision of Veronica, which had faded a few moments earlier, re-manifested itself, this time by my side.

'Oh, you're here,' I said, momentarily startled.

'Yes,' she replied. 'This is my work now. I look after – *and protect* – the city's sensitives, the children of today who are going to be tomorrow's mystics, clairvoyants and psychics.' And, with no more ado, she vanished again and I was left marvelling at what I had just seen and heard.

Two people with paranormal gifts – myself and the child in this world – and Veronica, a wise seer and mystic from the other world, had somehow, despite all the squalor, heat and pandemonium of our surroundings, managed to connect; and the communication with the child had bypassed the normal limitations of two people who spoke different languages. In truth, I had no way of knowing if the little girl had spoken to me in Italian or in English, which seemed highly unlikely in the circumstances, yet I had understood what she said. I didn't even know for sure if I had heard the words spoken aloud or as a spiritual sound that had emanated silently in my mind.

There were more surprises to come.

Later that evening when I was returning to my hotel, a very grim, medieval-looking place that had a small entry gate within a massive wooden door, I found myself walking alone down a street, which had cars and scooters parked on both sides. As I walked, I noticed a man coming towards me and, feeling instantly uneasy – *threatened* – I thought, 'Oh, Lord, what's he up to? What's going to happen?'

The next second, as the man drew closer, approaching me on my right-hand side, I sensed Veronica manifesting on my left side. Instantly inspired to link into her energy, I followed her lead as she led me in a weaving pattern in and out of the tightly parked scooters and cars, then along the side of the road. Aware that the man had nearly caught up and was now sprinting towards me, I launched into a final sprint myself and managed to push open the hotel's main door and hold it shut until, with a curse, he gave up and went on his way.

Back in the safety of my hotel room, I had absolutely no doubt that Veronica had protected me – saved me – from a brutal mugging by guiding me in and out of all the obstacles and barriers that had been placed between me and the safety of the hotel. The incident, I realised, had also taught me something about trust; that if we allow ourselves to respond to the positive energy that comes through from the other world, surrender ourselves to this universal power and allow ourselves to be at their command just for a moment or two, the enlightened beings will save us from potentially dangerous situations.

That meeting, then, with Veronica in the catacomb and later in the street, was a momentous event that was still occupying my mind when I arrived back in Essex. I felt then – and I still do – that, although ostensibly, I had gone to Naples to do some filming, I had also been *meant* to go there, that the journey was part of my present life's path. I have often found that being psychic is like living life one step ahead of events, and I remembered that I had felt unusually apprehensive at Stansted Airport on the day of my departure to Naples. When I actually focused on this feeling, I had had the sense that something extraordinary was going to happen to me in that legendary city that I had never visited before. And it had!

I had made a very special spirit friend during my stay there, a spirit friend who I had a strong affinity with, a spirit friend who had said: '*Know me, understand me, follow me, share with me my experience*', and a spirit friend who would certainly remain part of my life.

There was more.

I was also left with the feeling that, as well as protecting children herself, Veronica would help me when I was reading for parents whose children were psychic or had other special gifts, and also when I was involved with children who were sick or dying. Veronica, I felt, would be able to tell me things about the children and advise me on how best to guide them, especially children who are born with a 'higher knowledge'.

I am certainly sure that the little girl I met in Naples will grow up to be a mystic and that she will, perhaps, continue Veronica's good works – healing the sick and caring for the deprived.

II
Day by Day

Twenty-one years ago when I took my first tentative steps inside my local Spiritualist church, feeling very apprehensive and thinking I had a made a huge mistake, I never, for the life of me, thought that one day this work would play such a big part in my life.

During my first few months of attending the church, I sat there from the start to finish of the demonstration praying that the working medium for that night would *not* come to me. In fact, I used to have a secret plan that if the medium ever chose to swoop on me with a message from 'the other side' I would feign a coughing fit and ask to be excused. In the event, however, I never needed to put my secret plan into effect. Within those four walls, I felt such a sense of coming home – *belonging* – it was as if I had uncovered some great treasure trove that held within it all the answers to my life – and life itself.

As I sat there gazing at the ceiling in that tiny church I used to envisage a future where I would be so secure in my beliefs that I would spend all my days travelling the world studying the great teachers and philosophers and, most exciting of all, was the thought of being able to observe the world's greatest mediums at work.

'How amazing it is,' I thought, 'that these strange people, called mediums, can talk to the dead.'

For me, that was a *wondrous* thought and, to say the least, pretty cool!

Never in a million years, however, did I entertain the idea that one day I would be doing what they were doing, and the thought of being on television back then would have scared the wits out of me and probably propelled me prematurely into the spirit world! I was soon to discover, though, that everything happens for a reason and the Great Spirit has a way of taking your life in a different direction when you least expect it. In sporting arenas, I think this is called being thrown a 'curve ball'.

Well, one of my curve balls certainly came up when my friend and colleague, Colin Fry, arranged an introduction for me that led to my own television shows *Street Psychic* and *Psychic School*.

The exposure that these programmes brought me propelled my work to a whole new sphere, and introduced an entirely new audience to my work – people who had never been inside a Spiritualist church or centre. As a result, my work now takes me all over the UK and all around the world, giving me the opportunity to work in varied arenas demonstrating to people from all walks of life.

In 2005, when Colin and I embarked on our first joint UK tour, 'The Best of British', it was evident that we both had the same love of working for the spirit world, and we both felt totally honoured when we were able to pass on messages from loved ones who had passed.

To work as a medium, you must literally live your life between two worlds – our own physical world and that of the spirit world. Achieving this requires a great deal of focus and determination on the part of the medium, but also total support and sharing from those that surround and work with us. Because of our friendship, and because of the respect we have for each other's dedication to the work that we do, Colin and I are able to support each other and merge our psychic gifts to bring messages from loved ones to loved ones.

'The Best of British Mediumship' tour, then, was about two mediums, blending their energies and striving to do their best for members of the audience by passing on messages from those they loved who had gone on before them.

I love working with Colin. Such dates in my diary are always special, always have a plus-factor, and I remember an event that occurred a few days prior to our appearing at the London Palladium. On this occasion, I had been doing an EVP experiment with some of my students that had proved rather limited and I had only got one word on my tape recorder, a name which appeared about fifteen times, and the name was '*Judy*'.

After the session, I more or less forgot about this event, but I was in for a surprise when I got to the Palladium and was shown to the dressing-room that I was going to be sharing with Colin.

Having shown me in, the stage assistant said: 'D'you realise this used to be Judy Garland's dressing-room?' Then, as I began to focus and take in the surroundings, I could see that there were pictures of Judy all round the walls.

Remembering the puzzling EVP experiment, I couldn't help laughing out loud.

'Was it you, Judy?' I thought. 'Was it you trying to tell me that tonight I'd be occupying your space? Or was it the spirits just letting me know I should be feeling *very* honoured to share your dressing-room?'

Either way, I was thrilled to have received the tip-off during the experiment!

While we were working together on the tour, Colin and I went, among other places, to Bournemouth. On this occasion, we added a new element to the shows in which we took to the stage together in the second half to work on 'double links' – an attempt for both of us to link with the same spirit and then give the information we received to the intended recipient of the message.

In Bournemouth as we attempted this double link at the end of the show, it became evident that I was not picking up on the same spirit as Colin. Instead I had made a separate connection with a young man who was informing me that he had taken his own life.

I then had a very strong sense that he had been a very gentle man in life and that because of his hyper-sensitive nature he had found it difficult – *impossible* at times – to cope with everyday stresses and strains. As I continued to focus on him, he gave me other pieces of information that I hoped would help me to place him with someone in the audience, and my eyes were drawn to people seated at the back of the hall on the right-hand side. But as I finished relating the information he had given me, nobody in that area responded or claimed to know who this spirit could be.

'Tell her it was my second attempt,' he said.

As by now we were approaching the end of the show, and running out of time, I sent out an urgent prayer to my spirit guides to help me place the message.

At that moment, in my vision, the theatre darkened as if somebody had flicked off all the lights, and only one face, at the back of the auditorium on the right-hand side, stood out, shining as brightly as a beacon. There was no doubt in my mind that this lady was the intended recipient of the message, and I asked for a microphone to be handed to her. Very diffidently, she confirmed that she had recognised the spirit and the information he had given, but she had been too shocked, too moved and emotional to speak up.

As soon as I heard her voice, the spirit confirmed that the lady was his 'mum'.

There were two thousand people present in the auditorium

that night and I could not help marvelling that, despite the lady's understandable resistance, the spirit had overcome all difficulties to make his mother known to me.

This confirmed something that is frequently shown in my work, that when it comes to communication, there is nothing more powerful than the power of love to ensure a spirit gets through!

For one of my demonstrations, I returned to my roots in Canvey Island, Essex, where three hundred and fifty people packed themselves into Paddocks Hall to see me work.

From the moment I came on to the stage that night, the spirits made their presence felt. Messages came thick and fast as mothers, fathers, children and all manner of relatives and friends came through loud and clear. One contact that still stands out in my mind was a connection made with a young woman sitting at the front of the hall.

Having listened to a spirit, I said to her: 'I believe you have some connection with Fabergé eggs.'

'Oh, yes,' she replied, smiling. 'I paint them.'

'Your father's here,' I added, and I went on to give a detailed description of him and some more information that the lady accepted.

'He's telling me now that the spirits are trying to bring healing to a lady who is suffering acute pain in her right shoulder,' I continued.

Having looked blankly at me for a moment, the lady said: 'No, sorry, I can't place that.'

Unperturbed, I returned to the spirit and asked for some clarification.

'Apparently he is talking about Pam,' I said.

With that, the lady turned to the small group she was with and focused her attention on a rather shy, embarrassed-looking woman whose cheeks had turned bright red and who was looking down at the floor. Her name, it turned out, was Pam and, only moments before, she had said to another friend: 'I will have to go home soon because I am in such agony with my shoulder!'

What amazed me about this incident was not that the spirit knew that Pam was suffering and was able to pass on a simple message, but what I heard later in an email. Apparently the pain, which Pam had suffered from constantly for many years, had disappeared the moment she received the message and had not come back. That night the spirits had demonstrated their wondrous powers and worked a healing miracle.

During that same period, I was invited to take the mid-week service at Westcliff Spiritualist Church, a place I used to attend regularly a few years ago, and a place where I still work as often as my schedule allows.

From the moment I began to demonstrate, I felt over-shadowed by my spirit guides as I relaxed into one of the best demonstrations I have ever done there. Names, places and the most intricate pieces of information came through and, at times, I could hear the audience gasp. Finally, I went to a couple seated near the front of the church hall and described their son.

'His name is Paul Stephen and he is twenty-one years old,' I said.

The couple were *so* astonished, *so* delighted, they yelped out loud! As the message continued and their son passed on his love to them, I could see that, at long last, they had received the proof they had always longed for; that Paul, their beloved son, was still as much a part of their lives now as he ever was.

Turning my attention to a gentleman in the congregation, I said, 'Your mother is here and wants to send her love to her four sons.'

'She had *five* sons,' the man corrected.

'Yes, but only *four* are living and one is with her on the other side,' I answered, and he nodded his head in agreement.

Somewhere in my being, feeling sure I would receive the right information, I went out on a limb and asked the spirits for his dead brother's name. Then, hearing it as loud as if someone had just shouted it in my ear, I said, 'Peter.'

That, the man confirmed with great emotion, was the name of his brother who had passed.

Now, please do not think I am relating the stories in this book to boost my ego and increase your opinion of me. When the two worlds are able to merge, become as one, it is a triumph for the spirit world *not* for me. They do all the hard work, I am just the middleman. And, when everything comes together, I feel proud to be a part of a process that allows wonderful reunions between the two worlds, and I simply want to pass on what I have learned: that when people, spirit and medium pool their energies and pull together, anything is possible – and states of mind, lives, beliefs and hopes can be transformed in the twinkle of an eye.

While I was still thinking on these things, I did a demonstration in Gloucester. Midway through giving a message to a lady, I had a very clear vision that I knew was not connected with her. So, after taking a deep breath, I advised her that I would need to come back to her after I had told the audience what I had just seen.

'I have a young lady here who has long dark hair,' I announced. 'She tells me she was in her twenties when she passed after a long battle with cancer. She wishes to connect with two women, one of whom is her sister . . .'

Before I could say anything else, a hand shot up and began to wave frantically.

'Could you be her sister?' I asked.

'Yes – I'm *sure* it's my twin,' the lady replied through muffled sobs.

Detail after detail, regarding personal memories the twins had shared, confirmed this lady's statement to be true. Then, suddenly, I saw a clear image of a necklace and the spirit-sister impressed on me the following thought: 'She has my necklace here with her tonight.'

When I passed this information on to the living sister, she gasped.

'It's here in my hand,' she cried out. 'I'm holding it right now,' and she held up the necklace for all to see.

Now some sceptics may think, 'So, this was only a necklace', but just imagine the impact this detail had for the living twin who had sat holding it in the desperate hope that it would help her sister to make a connection with her in the packed auditorium. And how amazing that her wishes were picked up and acknowledged by the spirit-sister.

At the end of the demonstration the twin approached me and said: 'You can't *possibly* appreciate how much this evening has meant for me.'

But I did! The transformation that it had brought about in her was emanating from the very depths of her soul – was present for all to see.

No matter how long I have been doing this work, such moments still give *me* goose pimples!

It is not always like that! Sometimes it can be a hard task to get a message through to the correct recipient and not everyone is as eager to accept a spirit communication as the twin sister was that night. Likewise the ambience of a place is not always sympathetic to my work. When, for example, I was doing a demonstration in a hall not far from where I live in Essex, things did not go well. The hall, which was lit by fluorescent lights, was very bright and rather smelly from an overflowing drain next door. There were also lots of people in the audience who had never been to a demonstration of mediumship before.

At one point I was very aware that I was linking with the spirit of a young man, who was about seventeen when he passed very suddenly two years ago, following a motorcycle accident. He also gave me two names that were linked with him on earth. I found myself drawn towards a lady who I was sure was the recipient for his message. But when I offered her the information and asked if she knew this young man, all she kept saying was, 'No – no, I don't.'

Somewhat perplexed, I tried to see if anyone else would accept the information, but nobody seemed to know my seventeen-year-old spirit. He was *so* clear, though, it didn't seem right to send him on his way so soon, especially as he kept drawing me back to the same lady.

After much frustration – and just as I was about to give up – the lady suddenly said: 'Well, I do know of a seventeen-year-old who died in a motorcycle accident and, as it happens, he did have a connection to the two names you mentioned, but I never actually *knew* him. I only met him once.'

'Why didn't you say?' I asked gently.

'Because *you*,' she retorted accusingly, 'asked me if I *knew* him – and I *didn't* – not personally.'

At that point I could have screamed hallelujah, but I *didn't*!

After all, the lady wasn't to know how spirit messages work, and that it is not always the nearest and dearest of those who have passed who come close enough for a message. In such instances, a message can be given to somebody else to pass on. They become the medium's medium! All in all, that incident was a case of 'some things are sent to try us' and make us stronger, better workers!

A similar experience to the one above came to light when I

received the following letter from a very nice lady who obviously very much regretted missing an opportunity to communicate with her spirit family:

Dear Tony,

I barely know where to begin, but I feel compelled to write this letter and tell you of my experience when myself and seven other members of my family went to see you and Colin Fry in the Waterfront Hall, Belfast.

We were seated along the back row of the top tier and, as soon as we took our seats, I could feel a very cold draught of air passing between myself and my daughter, who also felt this. Then, when you came on stage, you began by saying you thought the first message was for someone at the back and you pointed to us. You then described my brother-in-law: how he died, at what age he passed, and you even said his name. All the details were so accurate that the eight of us knew it had to be his spirit that was with you. But not one of us moved. Then you went on to say that two days had passed before we found his body, which was also true. You also mentioned that you could feel another spirit-man alongside him and you went on to describe my dad. Once again, we were in no doubt that their spirits were with you, yet none of us said or did anything about it.

I am so sorry, Tony. We can't understand what happened. Moments later, I experienced a crushing pain in my chest which lasted throughout the rest of the show.

Really, I just want to say sorry. You have a wonderful gift and you work so hard to bring messages to people that spread so much happiness to so many, and I feel we let you down.

I am hoping that some day soon you will come back to Belfast and that this time one of us will find our tongue and be able to speak with you. In my heart, though, I think we probably missed our chance. So, once again, thank you, Tony.

Yours faithfully, Karen

If Karen was here at this moment, I would say: don't blame yourself for what happened! I have every sympathy for people who find themselves overwhelmed and unable to put up their hand in front of so many other people in an auditorium. There *is* something intimidating about being placed in the spotlight and handed a microphone when one is already feeling stunned to have been singled out by the spirit world.

What has to be remembered is that, like God the Great spirit, all spirits work in wondrous ways their miracles to perform. They are, I have discovered, very adept at the try-try-try-again syndrome, so there is never any reason to give up hope. If they have made one attempt, they will certainly make another!

During a demonstration in Dudley, I mentioned a communication that had just come through from the spirit world and, once again, nobody in the hall claimed it or seemed to know anything about it. The message concerned a young girl who had been abducted, bundled into the back of a car and subsequently murdered. As there was no response, I moved on to another communication. Later on in the evening, though, a man I had met on a previous occasion took the trouble to seek me out.

'I'm quite sure I know the identity of the girl you referred to,' he said. 'Some years ago I worked for a family whose teenage daughter was abducted and whose body was later found hanging in a drainage shaft.'

Later still, I also received a letter from a lady in which she wrote: 'I *really* wish I had spoken up at your demonstration when you were talking about the girl who was kidnapped. I believe it was a teenager who was found in a disused drainage shaft. I also believe that as I have never forgotten this poor girl and always made a point of remembering her in my prayers, that is *why* her spirit came through during your demonstration.'

During the next couple of weeks following this event, the spirit of a young girl appeared to me several times and each time she came she revealed more and more about the tragic events that had led up to her death. On one of her visits, I learned that her killer had kidnapped her after he read that she had inherited a huge amount of money. Then frustrated about the lack of progress he made when he tried to collect the ransom money, he had fallen into a blind rage and attacked her.

It really was an horrendous fate and the poor girl was not discovered until two months later. I was *so* distressed by all the things that she told me that I continued to hold her close to my heart and pray for her long after her spirit had ceased to feel the need to come to me.

The examples that I have outlined above are one reason why I no longer get flustered when people do not put up their hands or respond to messages I give out at demonstrations. The examples just go to show that while I am silently thinking, 'What's going on here?' the spirits are *not* misleading me, they *do* have a purpose and I must trust them even when I get a nil response at the time.

When, day by day, I am working away from home, which over the last few years has been more often than not, I often have *very* interesting and exciting paranormal experiences when I am least expecting them. These do not only occur when I am on stage or standing in front of a church congregation, my psychic awareness can be tingled and come into play at the most unexpected times; and occasionally these unexpected spirit contacts – paranormal encounters – can be astounding.

As mediums and psychics we are receptive to a number of influences in addition to, and way beyond, those which come from using the five senses: hearing, sight, taste, touch and smell. And, when we are working on a psychic level, we tune into the person we are reading for, feel their energy and assess what we are picking up from them in regards to the past, present and sometimes the future. No spirit contact is needed for a psychic message.

When we are working with mediumship, however, we blend with the other world and make connections with spirits. To help us in our work we can also at times link into residual energies, which allow us to connect with the memory of a past event that has occurred in a certain place: an event that has left an energy stain on the surroundings where it occurred. Imagine walking into a room where two people have just been having a heated disagreement. Even though this may now be over, we can still feel the awkward atmosphere and it is this 'imprinting' which gave rise to the old saying, 'you could have cut the atmosphere with a knife'.

If you then imagine what it would be like to walk into that same room after an event occurred, which involved emotions at the most extreme end of the spectrum, something really *unsavoury*, or *tragic*, or *wondrous* or *happy*, you will get an immediate understanding of *how* it is possible for really powerful emotions to leave a lasting impression in a place, an impression that seeps into the walls or the very fibre of the area where the events occurred.

When sensitives pick up on residual energies they are

sensing the memories of past events that are locked into the history of a place. It does not mean that they are picking up on the spirit of the person or persons involved in the incident. They are probably long gone but, nevertheless, what remains to be picked up is still very real and powerful. When, however, a sensitive is aware of a spirit in a place, this is because they are seeing, feeling or hearing a discarnate spirit who is trying to connect. The spirit is there in that moment in an endeavour to get a message through to those who are present. So, on occasions, it can transpire that we are not only picking up the residual energies deposited within a room, but linking to a spirit who was linked to the event – and this was something that happened to me very recently.

Oxford's New Theatre, with its rich plush interior and Victorian style architecture, is a beautiful building and quite something to behold. To enter it and take in its deep red cushioned seats, the splendid artwork painted on its tall cathedral-like ceiling, is like stepping back in time and it is one of my favourite theatres not only to admire but to demonstrate in.

During a recent visit there, as part of my 2005 tour, a member of the theatre's technical staff, approached me, saying: 'Is there any chance you could spare a moment after the show? There's some weird stuff going on upstairs and it's really starting to spook us.'

Now, this is not an unusual request for me to come across. I am often asked to go to buildings where the owners feel there is a presence, and I try to oblige as often I can, more to put their minds at rest than for any other reason.

So, when that evening's demonstration ended and after I had met a number of the audience who wanted to say hello, I went to investigate.

The small group that gathered for this visit consisted of the technician and his mate, my friend Stuart and four of the tour crew. Together, we started to climb a very tall staircase that took us towards the top of the building. At the top we were led into one of the old dressing-rooms, a dreary space that looked as if it had been long-since forgotten. As I had asked for the main lights to be switched off, only the light from the hallway lit the room.

Stuart and I walked in first, leaving the others to follow. I could tell they were all a little apprehensive and were only too happy for us to lead the way. I was not surprised! The whole area had a creepy feeling about it and Stuart and I were immediately sure we were being watched.

Suddenly, as we walked around the room, I was overcome with a gamut of emotions, which made me feel dizzy, nauseous and a little disoriented. I could also smell what I thought to be paraffin and suddenly the room seemed to grow very cold. The next moment I heard myself talking out loud to the group behind me, telling them what I was experiencing.

In my mind I could see an old-fashioned oil-lamp glowing in the corner and I could hear a voice speaking very softly and what sounded like someone crying. As I stood there desperately trying to make out what it was I was hearing, an overwhelming sense of panic started to arise in me and I wanted to scream and run out. Then I saw him.

I was actually standing looking into one of the many mirrors in the room but, instead of my own reflection looking back at me, there was the reflection of someone else.

His hair was black and his face, which was as white as the proverbial snow, appeared to be made of wax. The next moment I realised he had on thick theatrical greasepaint make-up. Wearing a large white shirt, with long flowing sleeves, and with one earring in his ear, he had a look of complete desperation and desolation stamped upon his features.

As I stared at the disturbing vision before me, I could see that he was crying, not just weeping but a deep mournful sobbing that filled my ears and took over my senses. Transfixed to the spot, I stood there totally consumed by his grief. Then I heard Stuart's voice at my side saying: 'Tony, can *you* see him? He's *crying*, can *you* see him?'

'Yes,' I replied.

At that, the man in the mirror turned and faced us, but rather than paying us any attention he stepped forward and walked straight through us. As I turned and followed him with my eyes, I saw him sit down at a dressing table and, still sobbing and seemingly unaware that he was being watched, he started to remove his make-up. Crossing the room, I sat down beside him. Then it happened.

For a moment I blended so completely with his mind that we became as one and, in that brief time, I knew that his pain and the utter void he was feeling was the result of unrequited love – the passionate love he had for another, the love he knew would never be returned. A young talented actor, with the promise of a golden future ahead of him, I also knew that his life had drained from him like wine from a bottle as, all in the name of love, he took his own life.

As I stood there, feeling his life-force drain away from him, I felt a little bit of me had been lost, too.

By this time, those around me were clamouring to hear what I had felt, what I had seen, and I endeavoured to relate all that had happened. But, after such an intense draining experience, it was difficult for me to concentrate and it took me quite a few minutes to return to a state of full awareness of my surroundings.

Before we left the room, Stuart and I discussed what we had seen in the shared vision which, in itself, was unusual and uncanny. Having done that, we decided to say a prayer for the poor man whose memories had been trapped in his dressing-room for so many years.

When the group eventually filed out, I was the last to leave. As I turned to take one last look at the lonely room, I heard his anguished cries for the last time before they softened and died away completely. I can only hope that *that* meant the prayers we had sent out for him that night had helped to release him and send him on his onward progression.

As I look back on this event now and recall the events of that evening, I am convinced that I was not only sensing the residual energies that existed within that space, but picking up on the spirit of a tragic gentleman who, for a brief moment in time, had connected with me to convey his story. It was as if he had wanted to get his story across to me in order to help him come to terms with the circumstances that had led him to that sad moment when he took his own life. And, as I acknowledged his presence and sent him my love, I truly believe that his spirit, which had so long been connected to that dreary place, felt a sense of healing and release.

'Day by day, spirits,' I said, as I closed my eyes that night, 'you continue to throw me curve balls – and *astound* me!'

Later still, thanks to this event, I found myself reflecting on love and all the joys and the agonies that it can bring us. It may sound curious – even erroneous initially – but those reflections led me to believe that we need to set boundaries to our love. This is *not* an easy feat because the temptation, of course, is to give whatever is asked of us and then, when asked, to give more, *give our all*, until we find ourselves exhausted – drained.

It is only when we set boundaries, though, that we will be able to avoid this situation and grow in respect – perhaps even be grateful – for the boundaries of others. The truth is that where people we love are concerned, our needs can grow and grow, until the loved ones become so overcome and overwhelmed by our needs they are practically forced to withdraw from us for their own survival.

One of our tasks, then, in life, is to claim ourself for *ourself*. Only then can we retain a sense of proportion and not expect from others more than they feel able to give. True mutuality in love requires people who remain in possession of themselves and their own identities while giving to each other. So, in order to give more effectively – and to be more self-contained where our needs are concerned – we must learn to accept that setting boundaries to our love is *positive* and can be a life-saver!

12
Touching People's Lives

For mediums, the bringing of the good news that there is life after death, that we can 'speak' to our loved ones, is the main purpose of our work, but passing on messages that offer guidance on current day-to-day matters or future events that may be worrying or distressing people are also common. The purists among us criticise any mention of future events as 'fortune-telling' and prefer their fellow mediums not to discuss anything to do with these.

Although I do not usually go in for prophecies in my work or speak of events to come, *if* I feel the spirit world is *urging* me to pass on certain information, or *if* what I am receiving is so strong that I feel I have no choice, I do from time to time offer this type of information to the person I am reading for.

I have always refused, however, to become a fortune teller or allow my work to go in that direction. In fact, when a man or woman comes for a private consultation and turns out to be only interested in knowing if they will meet that 'tall, dark, handsome stranger' or if their business will go from strength to strength and be more profitable next year, I usually inform them that I am *not* the medium for them, and urge them to go and see somebody else. I would much rather spend the time at my disposal reuniting families and bringing through evidence of continued survival.

On occasions, however, I do go with the flow and trust that what is coming through at that moment has to be said, and pass it on. In such instances, the message may be about a relatively insignificant event, such as a change of job or moving house, but it may also be a matter of life and death.

Sometimes, for example, when I am reading for an individual, I become aware that the spirit is concerned about the person's general health or a specific health condition. One instance of this was when I was reading for a middle-aged lady in a room I use for such purposes near my home. After I had given what I hoped was an acceptable reading involving spiritual communication, my attention was drawn to the left side of the lady's chest.

'Have you ever,' I enquired tentatively, 'had any problems or pain on the left side of your body, possibly under your arm?'

'No,' she replied emphatically. 'I haven't.'

At this point I must add that psychics and mediums have to be very careful indeed not to alarm anybody, or give medical advice, because we have not been trained to do so. For this reason, if I ever sense there is a problem, I always suggest that the person should make an appointment to see their GP.

And because, despite the lady's answer, I still felt that there was a problem on the left side of her chest, that's exactly what I decided to suggest on that day.

'Do me a favour, darling,' I said. 'I don't know what the problem is – and it is probably nothing – but, *please*, indulge me by making an appointment with your doctor and asking him to examine you. This would put your mind – and my mind – at rest.'

'All right,' she replied smiling. 'I will.'

Some time later I received a letter from her saying that she had gone to see her doctor, that he had given her a check-up, but he had found nothing wrong. So convinced was she, though, that the spirits could be right, she had asked her doctor if she could have a second opinion. Somewhat disgruntled by her request, he had implied that she was making a fuss about nothing.

'Why on earth do you want a second opinion?' he said.

Too embarrassed to say that she had been to see a clairvoyant, she simply replied: 'I just have a hunch that all might not be well.'

When she did get a second opinion, she was in for a shock.

'There is some evidence of the early signs of breast cancer,' the consultant informed her.

This was subsequently treated and I am delighted to say that, to this day, the lady is happy, well and clear of cancerous cells.

This, I believe, highlights the fact that clairvoyants do occasionally see things that need attention now or in the future. I cannot emphasise enough, though, that in our work we have a responsibility not to overstep the mark and interfere with people's lives. Our job is simply to present what we sense and, if there is a problem, suggest that they seek medical attention. It certainly remains my firm belief that on that day, when the spirits alerted me to the problem on the left side of the lady's chest, that they saved her life.

When I was developing my gift of mediumship from the age of seventeen onwards, it was all *very* exciting, wondrous and magical, and I can confirm that nothing has changed! If I have learned anything during my working tours and demonstrations, it is a coming to the understanding that there is an immense need in the people I demonstrate for regardless of age, race, creed or sex. There is so much grief, pain and anguish in every village, town and city I visit that there is an intense pressure to 'deliver the goods' to those in the audience who are hoping and praying that tonight will be the night when they receive proof that their loved ones have not gone forever.

I have to confess that it can be pretty daunting – and scary – at times to have such a weight resting on my shoulders, especially when I am demonstrating, night after night, to large expectant crowds.

Each night before I go on stage, I pray that I will be the best vehicle I can for the spirits to work through and bring messages and solace to those in need. However, I am not relating this because I am looking for sympathy, but because I am hoping that any potential mediums, who are reading this book and toying with the idea of starting on this journey, will go ahead at full speed. Why? Because, one day, when they have given their first message from a son to a mother, or husband to a wife, or a brother to a sister, and so on and so forth, they will have the deep satisfaction of knowing what it is like to touch someone's life in a very special way – and they will feel totally humbled and privileged in their chosen work.

Recently, while I was on tour, a young lady asked, 'What is the difference between a medium and a psychic?' And: 'Is it possible for anybody with an interest in the paranormal to develop a psychic gift or become a medium?'

'A medium,' I replied, 'is someone who is in touch with the next world and who is able to communicate with the spirits. A psychic is an individual who is blessed with the ability to "read" people's past, present and future. A medium can be doubly blessed and have both mediumistic and psychic talents, in which case he is called a psychic medium. A psychic, on the other hand, may be blessed with only one gift – extra sensory perception (ESP) – which is not attributable in any way to the spirit world.'

To a certain extent, I do believe that everyone is psychic, but only a few seek the appropriate guidance that will help them to develop what is essentially an innate sensitivity and gift.

When it comes to mediums, however, I believe they are

predominantly born not made. It takes phenomenal determination and courage to go out on a limb and embrace eternity, and ask questions that have puzzled mankind from the beginning of time and not all mediums go on to develop their gift to its full potential.

Those that do, however, are lucky to be alive today. We are living in an amazing period when it is totally acceptable to say, 'I am a developing medium' without causing mayhem. And, who knows, perhaps one day, thanks to our work and the work of others, every person on the planet will have received undeniable proof that death as a finality is the biggest lie we have ever been told and that, in truth, life is continuous.

It was with this hope of spreading the word in mind that I became the co-founder of the Avalon Project, a group I run for people who have an interest in mediumistic and spiritual matters. Now, after five years of organising courses and workshops, I am delighted to say that many of the novices, who attend the various groups, are now about to take, or have already taken, their first steps towards working in public for spirit.

At one of Avalon's annual development seminars at Eastbourne, I hosted a group for the advanced students. Most of these had been developing their gift for a number of years and most had attended many workshops. On this occasion, I was thrilled to see the transformation that had come about in some of them and I can honestly say that the standard of mediumship that they had reached was truly fantastic.

In one of the classes we worked at strengthening the spirit links when working with departed relatives, and then took turns to 'read' for each other at a deeper soul level. When mediums tune into the person they are reading for on a one-to-one basis, it is amazing what revelations can emerge. Information can come through, for example, on what our life path is intended to be; what lessons we need to learn while we are in this embodiment; and what baggage – unfinished business – we have brought back with us from previous incarnations and why.

This type of reading is totally therapeutic and can bring about a significant degree of healing. Soul readings can touch a person at a very deep level and bring to the surface many burdens that need to be released so that further progress can be made.

There is so much more to mediumship than many realise; a wealth of knowledge just waiting to be tapped. For me, the joy of such occasions is the knowledge that, thanks to the efforts the students are making and their unstinting willingness to listen and learn, the weight of pain and grief in the world will be that much lighter.

On one occasion I was very touched by a lady called Dawn Hutchins who I had first met on my television show, *Psychic School*, and who was now attending one of my seminars. Asked to give a talk to the group as part of an exercise, Dawn proved to be an inspiring speaker. She began by saying how privileged she felt to be on the path of development, and how unworthy she had felt when she was chosen for *Psychic School*. As she finished her talk, she spoke of the legacy she would like to leave when the time came for her to depart from this earth.

'I won't have anything of great financial value to leave to those I love,' she said. 'No diamonds or pearls, or cash or property, but, because of this, I want to make an extra effort every day to touch someone's life in another way. This may entail picking up the phone, even if I am tired, to make a call to someone I have not spoken to in a while; or offering a few kind words to a stranger at a bus stop; or lending an ear to a person in need; or paying a compliment to someone whose confidence needs a boost. All this – *and more* – is the legacy I hope to leave. And this will be my way of leaving something of *real* value behind, my way of saying thank-you for all the blessings I have received in this lifetime.'

I think we could all take something of great value from what Dawn said that day and, if we follow in her footsteps, we, too, could play our part in touching others' lives as she is doing. *That*, for me, is the essence of spirituality and the great bonus is that as we transform the lives of others, however briefly, we transform our own lives, too. God truly does work in mysterious ways His wonders to perform!

A few questions that follow me around when I am teaching or conducting seminars are:

'How is it that no matter how hard I try, I can never receive a message from the spirit world? I feel spirit beings around me, but I never seem to get a personal connection with them.'

My answer usually goes along the following lines: 'Being able to receive messages at will is something that can take a while to develop, but the most important aspect is to remain open to the possibility that it can happen. If you are already feeling their presence, it is likely that you are already picking up information from spirit beings without being aware that you are doing so.

'Spirit communication is a two-way process. When you feel spirit beings come close to you, acknowledge them mentally by thinking, "I know you are there" or "Thank you, friends, for coming so near". This will encourage the spirit personalities and let them know that their efforts are being appreciated and recognised.'

It is important to appreciate that the messages and impressions that come through to us from the spirit world are very subtle at times, and that it is necessary to clear the mind of clutter in order to be able to recognise what they are offering. Reaching a relaxed, meditative state of mind through listening to recorded meditations, or by focusing on ingoing and outgoing breaths, will clear the mind of random day-to-day thoughts, such as paying the bills, shopping, housework and so on, and put you in the right frame of mind to become a channel for messages to flow in and out.

Once potential mediums have opened themselves up in this way, the spirits may require them to help bring messages of hope and continued survival to those around them. If so, there may come a time when the would-be medium will need to take their development a step further and join a group or attend a suitable development workshop. Spiritualist churches often have development circles and groups, and the nearest can be checked out to see what is on offer.

Sharing in the power generated by a group really accelerates development as does the support from fellow students and the guidance from tutors.

If the person then decides they truly wish to become a medium, a great deal of dedication and commitment will be required. The rewards, however, are immense. Working with the power of the spirit is a true blessing.

'Why is it,' new students of the paranormal sometimes ask, 'that so many of the messages that mediums pass on to people from the spirit world are so mundane? Surely spirits have more important things to convey than to waffle on about Aunt May's wonderful jam tarts or Uncle Jim's prize dahlias?'

'Progressing into the higher realms,' I answer, 'does not mean that we lose our individuality and become entirely different characters who are unrecognisable to everyone except the spirits we now live among. We may have departed from earthly life, but we continue to be ourselves – our own true selves – and if our friends, who are still living, are to recognise us, then we must present evidential information that they will connect with us. If I was a rough-and-ready character in real life, my living relatives will not know me if I come through speaking in a very erudite way and quoting W.B. Yeats or some other poet. Just as *you* are still *you*, I am still *me* – and no one else. And, for this reason, you and I will still know and recognise each other, just as you know and recognise your relations and friends on earth.

'And, in the eternal future that stretches before us all, regardless of whether or not we believe in the afterlife, we will not be lost to those who were our joy and our solace while we were on earth.'

'Why,' others persist, 'is a sense of humour so lacking in the messages that come through from the spirit world?'

'That is *not* my experience!' I reply. 'On the contrary. Many of the spirits I have dealings with in my work have a sense of fun and seem to enjoy sharing a good laugh. In fact, I often end up having a fit of the giggles.'

On one occasion, for example, when I was giving a message to a niece from her aunt, I had a very strong vision of about half-a-dozen pairs of very large ladies' knickers billowing about on a washing line with some equally large pillowcases next to them.

'I can't imagine *why* she's showing me this,' I exclaimed to the niece, 'but I'm *not* kidding. I am seeing knickers and pillowcases – and the knickers are huge.'

'Well, she was a big lady,' the niece laughingly replied.

With that, I saw each pair of knickers being carefully placed inside a pillowcase. Having passed this information on to the niece, I said, mystified: 'What on earth is this about?'

When she had got over laughing, she replied: 'It's the most *wonderful* piece of evidence you could have given me. When my aunt was alive, she had an absolute thing about putting on a pair of fresh clean knickers every day but, because she was *so* big and her knickers were *so* large, she was embarrassed and couldn't bear anybody to see them hanging on the washing line. So she always put them out to dry inside a pillowcase!'

It was a *really* lovely moment. The niece was tickled pink and left in no doubt that it was the spirit of her auntie who had come through; and I could feel the aunt's pleasure that she had succeeded in making her presence felt.

What I am trying to convey here is that I am quite sure that if a sense of humour was a natural part of a person's character while they were here on earth, then they take it with them to the spirit world, and continue to express themselves in this way when communicating with their loved ones.

Having said that, I do sympathise with what lies behind the lack-of-humour question. I am only too aware that humour is a subject that is often sadly missing in religious writings and deliberations about the afterlife, and that a sense of fun and love of laughter often appears to belong exclusively to those living on earth. It is as if many people believe that our sense of humour dies with our physical body and is cast off, abandoned forever, before we reach the spirit world. In my experience, however, nothing could be further from the truth. So, let me reassure everybody, here and now, that whatever sense of humour we may have possessed while here on earth will be retained and will be just as much in evidence when we pass into the spirit world.

Other people I meet are interested in finding out who their spirit guide might be.

'It's my belief,' I say, 'that spirit guides are often old friends and relations. If you accept the idea of reincarnation, maybe some are even from other lives before this one. As such, spirit guides can be far easier to connect with than people realise because there is already such a strong love bond.

'The first step is to give them permission to come close and to let them know you want to be aware of them. We often wonder why spirit beings do not talk to us, but sometimes we forget to talk to them!

'Our guides have great respect for our free will and privacy, and need to know we are ready to receive them. Over a period of time a connection will be made.

'We may, for example, feel him or her in dreams, clairvoyance, clairaudience or just have an overwhelming knowing feeling when they are present.

'The important thing is to take time to get to know them, maybe asking why they guide us, why they agreed to work with us throughout this life and try to learn more about them and their life when they were on this earth.

'It's a case of the guide and the guided, so imagine how wonderful it would be for them to know you recognise and appreciate them, and want them to draw close to you.'

Pets are another favourite topic of conversation. 'They give us such unconditional love,' people say, 'that I would love to believe that they continue to exist in the other world. What do you believe?'

I have always thought that there is so much we can learn from our pets about love. Whatever our situation in life, whether we live in comparative luxury or poverty, and whatever our mood or state of mind, they love us just the same. And, *yes*, I do believe they exist in the afterlife and, indeed, I have seen spirit animals many times.

'Each animal, like each human, has its own character and personality and each is endowed with consciousness and I believe, like us, they can develop spiritually. Spirit, in whatever form it takes, is indestructible and I can honestly say that I get as much joy out of reuniting people with their pets as I do in reuniting them with their friends and relatives.'

I am certainly convinced that my much-loved dog who died a couple of years ago, will be waiting to jump up at me, wag her tail and lick my hand when we meet again on the other side! I am not quite sure, though, what she would make of the dog I now have, my Border Terrier, Archie, as they are as different as chalk and cheese. She was a demure lady and quite a snob, who took to very few people. Archie, on the other hand, is rough-and-ready and into everything and anyone who pays him the slightest attention. Anyone who claims animals do not have their own unique personalities should, perhaps, take time to explore this a little further!

One example of an animal making its presence felt occurred recently when I was doing a demonstration in a theatre at Salisbury. Having just finished one message, I looked to both sides of me to see if I could feel the presence of a man or woman wishing to communicate, but all I could see was a chimpanzee dressed in a little blue-and-white striped top.

'Excuse me, ladies and gentlemen,' I said, sounding almost as tentative as I felt, 'but I have a chimpanzee here who is making it clear he's hoping to make connect with someone who knew him.'

All this, of course, was greeted with an assortment of sniggers and laughs and nobody put their hand up.

'Strange though it might appear to all of you,' I persisted, 'animals do communicate with mediums by thought transference, and this chimp's thoughts are very clear to me. He's saying over and over again: "I was in the circus and I'm looking for someone who knows me."'

At that moment a lady, sitting at the end of an aisle on the right-hand side of the theatre, put up her hand.

'Do you know this chimpanzee?' I asked.

'I *do*,' she replied. 'I'm sure he belonged to my mum. She

had this chimpanzee, who had once lived in a circus, and when he retired he came to live with her.'

With that, the chimpanzee raised his paw so that I could see he was holding the hand of a lady, who was standing just behind him in spirit. That lady turned out to be the mother of the lady in the audience and, having been acknowledged, the mother was then able to pass on a very simple loving message to her daughter.

What interested me about that incident was that there were so many people in the audience who were hoping to receive messages from their mothers – and doubtless so many spirits who wanted to come through – but that particular spirit-mother had hit upon the idea of sending her little friend, the chimpanzee, to catch my attention and bring her to the fore. Often, in our circles, we talk about spirits who are 'enablers', who, just for a few minutes, enable another spirit to butt in. And, on this occasion, it was the little chimpanzee who played this role for that mother.

'As you have such close contact with the other side,' one man said to me, 'I am wondering if you are affected in the same way as other people by the death of a loved one?'

'I grieve in exactly the same way as others,' I replied. 'And rue the fact that my loved ones are no longer here with me on earth. But, having said that, my burden is greatly lightened as I still have contact with them in the other world.'

'Given what you believe about the afterlife,' he added, 'are you afraid of dying?'

'No,' I replied. 'But I am afraid of the method of dispatch! It may be simple, it may not. I am no hero and no more keen on suffering than anybody else. This aside, though, I am very much looking forward to returning to the other world.'

'What does it feel like to die? And do you have any sense of what the moments immediately after are like?'

'I can only say that throughout all the years I have worked as a medium, I have never come across a spirit who has described the act of dying as frightening, something we need to fear, and this has been just as true of the spirits who have died in accidents, committed suicide or been murdered as it is of people who died in more natural ways.

'Some mediums, who have sat with those who are dying, have described how, at the moment of death, the person's spirit – soul – exits through the crown of their head and that a great sense of calm, peace, light and presence fills the atmosphere, followed by a sense of the spirit of the person having vacated the room and been collected.

'I have also gleaned from spirits that, soon after death and after the new arrival has been welcomed by their loved ones who have previously passed, that there is a transition period, a period of adjustment. Then, having survived death, it is only natural that the spirit wants to convey this to those left behind.'

The simple truth, then, that I have found in my work is that some spirits, according to their character, need to go through a period of adjustment while they come to terms with what has happened to them and get to know their new surroundings; and that others make a quick recovery and want to make contact with those still on earth as soon as possible.

Finally, however desperate a living, grieving relative may be to make a quick contact – and however hard a medium may try to help – communication will not be possible until the spirit is ready to take this step. However long it takes, though, I have *never* doubted that the spirits remain inextricably bound to those they have loved in life.

I was very moved by one lady student who said: 'When my brother was very near the end of his life, I remember sobbing aloud and saying to him, "If you can, will you come to me when I am on my deathbed, dying?" Through his tears, he replied: "Heaven would have a job to hold me and as for Hell, I'll break it into tiny bits if it gets in my way." Do you think,' she added, 'that he will be there?'

'*Yes*,' I replied. 'The kind of bond you had with your brother is *eternal*. You have *not* lost each other and, in one shape or another, one relationship or another, throughout your lives, you and he will always be there for each other. He is part of your soul group and you are part of his. His death, painful though it is for you, is a transitory state, an interruption, and you will be reunited.'

To sum up what is a very natural fear of dying, I would like to add that when I was a child I used to try to imagine what it would feel like to be *nothing*, which is how the majority of us regard death. Lying in bed or on the grass in the garden, I used to close my eyes and screw up my face as tightly as I could while I tried to experience what it would feel like to be without sight, hearing, taste, touch or smell, and floating in an endless pitch-black sea of nothingness.

It was a strange, scary, even petrifying sensation at times, which continued to fascinate me for a couple of years. Somehow, though, I always sensed that this was *not* our destiny; that death was *not* nothingness; that there was an afterlife that, although different from life, was every bit as rich and as vibrant as life itself.

I have never ceased to believe that; and one of the bonuses of this belief is that it not only changed my attitude to death, it changed my attitude to life. I became aware, for example, that I was not troubled or restricted by the feeling that we shouldn't risk taking too many chances with the life that we have been given because we might lose it – and *that* will be *that*.

On the contrary, the belief in the afterlife, that there was *much*, *much* more to come, liberated me, allowed me to be bolder, more adventurous, go out and take more chances. I no longer lived with the fear that we only live once, and I had to be cautious and cling on, come hell and high water, to what I had.

Instead, I learned, along with others who shared a belief in the afterlife, that the fact that there were endless possibilities meant that we could keep all our options open and when life presented a challenge that may have a whiff of danger, we need not shrink back in fear. Instead, we could say, *YES*, and meet the challenge head-on.

I do realise, of course, that there is another side to believing that we only have one life; that it can have the opposite effect from liberation: that some people, who believe we only live once, feel totally driven and compelled to pack as much into it as possible, and this is done with no consideration for anybody else's feelings, because there is no time for such niceties and this life is seen as the be-all-and-end-all of existence. *That* state of mind is very different from feeling free to remaining open to life because we know there are many more chapters and opportunities to come. One belief allows for a joyous existence, the other is a fear-driven, frantic way of carrying on.

One of the reasons I feel blessed in the work that I do is that experience has taught me which belief system to trust, which to value, and every time I think on these things all I want to do is to touch other people's lives and share with them what I have learned by shouting over and over again from the rooftops: '*We cannot die. Life is eternal!*'

13
Bless you, Spirits

Recently, when I was asked to give a demonstration of mediumship at the College of Psychic Studies in South Kensington, London, it turned out to be a *really* interesting evening. The college has a large meeting room, which seats around one hundred and fifty people, and on this occasion it was packed to capacity. The evening went well, the spirit people were clear and I had no problem whatsoever in connecting with the other world. Message after message, each full of evidence and charged with emotion, flowed through me.

As I started on yet another message, I was aware of two spirit people connecting with me, who were husband and wife in life.

'We died in a fire,' they told me, and then indicated that they wanted to connect with a woman near the back of the hall.

As I couldn't quite see where they were directing me, I gave out the information and asked if anyone at the back recognized these two people and the circumstances surrounding their death. To my dismay nobody answered.

What I was 'seeing' and 'hearing', though, was *so* clear I knew I had to stick with it. So, I asked my spirit guides to help me find the intended recipient(s) of the message by giving me more information.

Moments later, I heard the name 'Elizabeth' called out simultaneously with the word 'nana', and I was very drawn to a lady who was seated near the back of the hall, the place I had originally wanted to go to.

'Does the name Elizabeth mean anything to you?' I asked.

'Yes,' she replied, visibly startled. 'Elizabeth was the name of my grandmother – my nana.'

It was obvious the lady was absolutely delighted to receive a message from her long-lost relatives and, as the spirit communication continued, my spirit guides then showed me a vivid image of a star of David and, as I saw this, I understood that there must be a strong Jewish connection. Then, in my mind, I was shown a large factory where there were animal pelts hanging on hooks. Then I heard the word 'furriers' and the name 'Cohen'.

'That's *amazing*!' the lady replied when I gave her this information. 'My nana, Elizabeth, worked at a furrier's in the East End of London and the man and woman, who owned the shop, were Jewish and their name was Cohen. They were a lovely couple,' she added, 'and my nana used to take me to see them sometimes. These visits only stopped when the factory burned down and they died in the fire.'

As a ripple passed through the audience, the lady twigged what she had just said.

'Oh,' she gasped. '*Of course*. I didn't make the connection earlier – I didn't realise!'

This, I feel, just goes to prove as it has on so many occasions, that when the spirits want to get a message through, they will succeed, even if we have to go round the houses for a while to get there!

Along with the original communicators, I was able to bring some more of the lady's family through.

'I have a baby boy here,' I said at one moment. 'A baby who passed on when he was about nine months old.'

'I know who that is,' the lady replied excited.

'It's your brother, isn't it,' I replied.

'Yes,' she answered. 'He was just ten months old when he passed.'

She was, of course, thrilled to hear from her baby brother and there was absolutely no doubt that the evening had answered a real need in her, and had contained some life-changing moments that would remain with her for all time.

As I said earlier in the book, working at the London Palladium was an amazing experience, one I treasure and shall never forget. Walking out on to a stage where so many of theatre's greatest names have performed was a very special humbling experience.

Before I went there, I had wondered if the spiritual presence of so many of the great and famous would linger on in the wings of that theatre and on that well-trodden stage and, perhaps, inhibit my performance, but I need not have worried. The airwaves were not too crowded and, as I faced an auditorium filled to capacity with a few thousand people greeting me with whistles and thunderous applause, I was immediately aware of a woman's spirit at my side.

I could tell she was a lady in her late thirties, possibly early forties, when she passed into the spirit world. I got the feeling she went with a cancer-related illness, and that she tried very hard to fight her illness and stay longer with her mum and other members of her family. When I told the crowd that she was drawing my attention to two photos and wanting to get a message to her mum, at that moment, a lady's hand had shot up. When I asked her whether she recognised the person, her voice was breaking as she answered that she did.

'Well, my spirit-lady wants you to know that she is okay, really happy and that she knows you have been looking at two photographs of her today.'

'Yes – *yes*, that's absolutely right. I was looking at them this morning.'

'I feel that she was ill for several years before she passed, that things had not been right for quite a long time. Does that make sense?'

'Yes – *yes*, it does!'

'She wants to thank you for being there with her when she died, and for holding her hand as she passed out of this world into the next and she's making it clear that you were sitting on her left-hand side when you said goodbye.'

'Yes, *that's right*, I was.'

'She's telling me that although she was in a coma for three days, she doesn't want you to think that she was suffering because she *wasn't*. By then, she was far away from all the pain and discomfort.'

Having paused to listen some more, I asked the lady in the audience: 'Do you remember placing a flower on her hand?' She looked rather shocked but told me that she absolutely had done that.

'Well, she is saying that she was *longing* to give it back to you as a farewell present.' I paused. 'She is now mentioning a ring. Are you wearing her ring?'

At that moment a younger lady sitting next to the lady I had been talking to reached for the microphone and told me that she was my spirit-lady's older sister and that she'd put the ring on that morning. In fact she was wearing it at that very moment.

'Bear with me,' I said. 'Because my lady is now saying that she wants to ask about a young girl of about eleven or twelve years of age.'

'*That's her daughter.*'

'Right. Has her daughter recently had some eczema on her tummy?'

'Yes – *yes*, she had.'

'Well, my lady is conveying that, although she knows you are doing your absolute best, her daughter needs some extra attention for that.' Having paused again, I added: 'Can I have your mum back for just a moment.' And, once the mother was holding the microphone again, I said: 'I gather you have felt your daughter's physical presence by your side when you are lying in bed and that sometimes you felt the end of the bed creak and the mattress sink a little as if somebody had sat on the edge of the bed. Is that so? Has that ever happened to you?'

'Yes,' the mother gasped. 'Yes, several times.'

'Well, your daughter is now saying: "That was *not* your imagination, mum, that *really* was me in the room with you."'

Pausing to listen a moment longer, I added: 'Darling, have you or was it your daughter who suffered with her throat? I ask because all the time I have been working with you I have felt a restriction in my throat and found it almost impossible, to swallow and now that your daughter is leaving us, I feel as if I am gagging. What does this mean?'

At that moment, her sister grabbed the mike and said: 'She had *thyroid* cancer.'

A gasp rippled through the auditorium, followed by a stunned silence that was only broken by a round of applause.

Later that evening when the mother and daughter were interviewed in the foyer of the theatre, they were clearly so moved by their experience. They spoke of the comfort it had given them to have confirmation that their gorgeous, loving relative had moved on to the spirit world.

I also found it moving and I was so glad for them. Throughout the entire communication I had been very conscious that there was a lot of love in that family, and I was *so* thrilled that the daughter's spirit had been able to come forward and convey so much evidence of her identity. It was a truly memorable event for me and the family.

When I was waiting in the wings of the Palladium just before I was due to go on stage for the second half that evening, I prayed that I would be able to make another good link with the spirit people – and my prayers were answered.

As the welcome-back applause dwindled away and I stood looking down at the sea of expectant faces I felt a man at my side who was in his fifties when he passed. I wanted to place him with somebody who was about twenty-six years of age when he went over. I could tell that my man was a good, family-orientated man and that his passing came suddenly, and I was aware of a constriction in my chest, that made me suspect that he died of a heart-attack. I was relating to the audience as I was listening to him and when I mentioned that there were four people who watched him leave this life and that he wanted to be connected with his daughter who was in the audience, suddenly a lady's hand went up.

'I think this is your father in the spirit world. Do you understand that there were *four* people who were present with him as he went?'

'*Yes* – I am one of four.'

'Did your father have blue-grey eyes?'

'*Yes* – he did.'

'Well, he has just winked at me and I have a strong feeling that he had a cheeky side to his character. He was a very loving, happy man. I already know that you are one of four, but he is also indicating three young children as well.'

'That would be right. I have three children.'

'Good. He's now making it clear that he keeps his eye on them from the spirit world and that on those occasions when you can't watch over them, he does!'

Having listened again, I said, 'I do not feel that this gentle-man passed recently. I feel he passed some time ago and he wants to apologise for doing so at a time when you still very much needed him – your dad – to be around you. He also wants to make it clear that, although he couldn't make your second wedding, his spirit eyes saw all that went on.'

The young lady, who was visibly trembling, constantly nodded her head to confirm that all this information was correct.

'I know you were able to say goodbye to him,' I continued. 'But towards the end he was very breathless and unable to respond. He now wants to say what he couldn't say then, that he loves you, wants you to look after yourself and to know that he is watching over you.' Having paused, I added tentatively: 'I don't want to get too personal but, since your father has passed, I am getting the sense that there have been a lot of difficulties between you and a man in your life. Your dad is also making it clear that he couldn't stand this fellow.'

'He's talking about my first husband,' the lady called back. 'He *hated* him.'

'Yes. Well, I don't want to make out that your dad was a violent man, but he is also making it clear that if he was still alive he would have belted him!' Having waited until the laughter died down and the young lady ceased nodding, I added: 'Do you know somebody called Joanne, darling?'

'It's the woman my husband went off with.'

There was so much laughter after that remark, the communication came to a natural end!

Afterwards, when answering questions in the auditorium, the young lady spoke about her amazement at being picked out to receive a message and the level of concrete detail that I'd been able to provide. I was thrilled, as always to have been able to bring some comfort.

One way and another that evening at the Palladium produced some remarkable evidential readings, which was wonderful because the important thing about such occasions is that they do not only touch the lives of the people who are directly concerned with a message. The proof that is in the detail affects everyone present at a very profound level, and even the harshest of critics is hardpressed to dismiss it all as mumbo-jumbo.

One thing I know for sure is that when I am a wizened old gentleman, living out my sunset years in the proverbial rocking chair, I will look back on that night at the Palladium and a broad smile will cross my wrinkly old face as I recall that I once stepped out on that historic stage and was greeted with a rapturous applause that quite took my breath away!

'Pay attention to the detail,' we are always being told.

Over the years, it has become apparent to me that *that* piece of advice is as true in the spirit world as it is in life. The *proof* of eternal life, I could say, is so often presented in the detail, and I have never ceased to be amazed at how innovative the spirits are in conveying who they are. Many are the times when I find myself saying at the end of a reading or a demonstration: '*Bless you, spirits*. Ten out of ten for that. The information you brought us was *spot-on*, exactly what your family needed to hear.'

Now, as I begin to put the finishing touches to this book, I am recalling yet another special moment that occurred during a one-to-one reading for a lady named Becky. A young vivacious lady in her twenties, who had a very infectious giggle, Becky asked me to make a tape-recording of the reading I was doing for her. As soon as I sat down to begin the reading, Becky's mother, a vibrant woman only in her forties when she passed with cancer, came straight through.

Becky was obviously deeply moved and happy with the information I was able to pass on but, as the reading neared its end, I was hoping for one more piece of information, her mother's name, that I knew would be a very important piece of evidence for her.

Tantalisingly, although I kept asking my spirit guides for the name, they seemed to have their own agenda and it did not surface throughout the reading. Feeling somewhat disappointed, I started to bring the session to its natural close. However, as I leaned over to switch off the tape recorder, a spirit voice, as clear as the proverbial bell, spoke directly through me in a voice that was not my own.

'Christine,' it rang out. '*Christine*.'

As I looked at Becky, she seemed to have turned white and her mouth had dropped open.

'Oh my God, that's my mum's name,' she gasped. 'Her name was *Christine* . . .'

I very nearly repeated, '*Oh, my God*', because the voice had come out of the blue and had startled me. It was a strange experience, almost like speaking in my sleep.

I was *so* relieved for Becky, though. I knew she had found all the pieces of information I had given her important and reassuring, but nothing had topped hearing me say her mother's name. At that moment they were two ladies, mother and daughter, separated by physical death and yet reunited by the wonderful power of the spirits.

That's what I call a good day's work.

I know some people believe that peace of mind can lull people into a false sense of security, but I've always thought that one of its great virtues is that it increases our mental powers. In my experience the mind works a lot more efficiently when it is cool rather than overheated!

One useful way that I have discovered to free the mind is to set aside some time to place our habitual thoughts under the spotlight by writing them down and studying them. In this way we can establish whether we are being governed by any negative thoughts and, if so, replace them with thoughts which are much more conducive to a creative frame of mind. For example, if we have got into the habit of thinking, 'I *can't* do that', we can replace that sentence with, 'Well, I could give it a shot and see what happens!' Our life may not be transformed overnight but, given time and a dose of the try-try-try-again syndrome, a change will take place.

Whether we are aware of it or not every one of us forms, and then labours under, our own estimate of what we believe ourselves capable of achieving. And it is this estimate which determines what we become. In truth, we cannot be more than we believe ourselves to be. This is because beliefs, both negative and positive, have a phenomenal impact upon us.

So, before I bring this book to an end, I want to share a few closing thoughts with you. First and foremost, I want to say that whatever your goal is in life, you *can* attain it if you believe in yourself, and if you keep on believing even when you are up against all the odds. Anything is possible.

I am only too aware that there are millions out there who want to believe that there is more to life than we are born, we live and then we die, and I want to emphasise that, however long it takes to get your first glimpse of the Great Spirit at work in your life, or your first inkling that there is life after death, *persevere*. I have learned from long hard experience that if we believe something is beyond our reach, it will be; if we think we are beaten, we will be. But if we dare to stay the course and remain willing to go out on a limb, we will discover as I did that perseverance is everything and success is determined by will.

A long time ago a man called Robert Bruce, who had taken refuge in a dank, dark, inhospitable cave found himself watching one small miracle of nature, a spider weaving its web, and, as he did so, his mind took a quantum leap as he realised that life's battles don't always go to the strongest or the most fleet of foot. The man who is most likely to win is the man who thinks he can and is willing to *try-try-try-again*.

So, whatever our goal is in this life or the next; and however long it may take us to be reunited with those we have loved in this world or the next, I cannot think of a better philosophy for us to place our trust in while we wait than this *try-try-try-again* concept. And for all of you who are blessed with a psychic gift that you are hoping to develop, and for those of you who are already workers in this field, a word of advice: Be kind to yourself – pace yourself. Such work can be a blessing and a curse. To 'see' what others do not see is a great responsibility and, just like a sharp-edged sword the gift should be wielded with great care. To be a spiritual warrior, it is sometimes necessary to hold your shield high. Working with people can be difficult and negative, and sometimes the 'arrows' can pierce our very being. Likewise, the pressure to give of our best, be accurate and know all the answers can be a heavy armour to bear. But if we remain focused on the path of service – and give the credit where it is due, to our spirit friends – victory will be ours. Please trust me – I speak from experience!

As I have said on so many occasions I am lucky because I have never been one to worry about the sceptics or those who berate my work, and I do not feel it is my mission to convert them all.

'I don't have any desire to do that,' I explain. 'And, even *if* I did, I wouldn't have enough hours in the day to try.'

I have always thought this is the best response to those who are trying to needle me but, for some reason, it seems to aggravate my attackers when they realise they are not having a negative effect on me. They just cannot comprehend what it is like to have such a strong belief – and to be so resolute in a faith – that it is possible to remain unaffected by the 'sticks and stones', criticisms and name-calling.

Likewise, because I am totally at ease in my own beliefs, I am able to accept that there are many different belief systems, a million miles from my own, on this wonderful diverse planet of ours. And I am so glad I do not feel threatened by this diversity because when we are not happy to accept that we do not all think and feel the same, division and hostility can occur.

My view, though, is that if we believe one thing and someone else believes another, why should that matter, why should it cause conflict? We only do ourselves harm when we get wound up because others do not share our way of thinking. In my experience, to 'live and let live' and allow each person to have his or her own beliefs and faith, or none at all, is a good philosophy to live by!

Having said that, I obviously do feel that investing some time and energy into reflecting on the afterlife is well worth the effort. My guess is that most people reading this book will be believers or, at least, open to the possibility that there is life after death. If, by chance, however, any sceptics are dipping into these pages, I would like to say: 'Imagine what a huge impact it would have on your life if, having invested some time in the subject, you came to believe that there was more to us humans than flesh and blood. How mega life-changing a concept that would be – and what could be more worthy of a little time and investigation?

'If someone was to tell you that there was a million pounds at the bottom of your garden, even though the possibility seemed ridiculous and beyond all reason, I am sure you would feel the need to pop down and have a look when nobody was around! What I am asking you to consider, however, is worth more than a million pounds, is worth all the money in the world, and at least deserving of a second glance, an open-minded enquiry.

'If, after you have delved into the subject by reading spiritual books, watching mediums at work, and visiting churches of every denomination, you still do *not* believe, then at least you will know you have come to an *informed* decision. If you then take no further action, we will all just have to accept that going through life *without* acceptance is obviously right for you this time round. But no worry. Perhaps we'll get you next time!

'If, on the other hand, your studies encourage you to continue until you embrace eternity, you will never be the same again; you will never feel alone; and you will approach death in a totally different way. Your life will also zoom from black-and-white to glorious technicolour, and you will learn to appreciate everything around you and view creation with a sense of awe and wonder.

'This does *not*, as I can confirm, involve becoming perfect overnight and living thereafter a demure, pure 'holier than thou' life. Along with many of us, I enjoy a party and I am prone to using some colourful language. Behind all these superficial things, however, is a *firm* foundation, a feeling that my house is *not* built on shifting sand, and a strength to cope with everything that life lays at my feet; and the courage to recognise my faults and weaknesses; and the will to dust myself down and try again when I realise I have made a mistake.

'So, let me confirm for one last time that being one of the lucky ones who acquire a belief system – *a faith* – does not prevent us from living life to the full. In fact, life becomes *fuller*! And I highly recommend everybody to think of each day, each minute, even each second as a gift, and to use the allotted time to seek out new adventures that stretch the mind and help us to fulfil our potential as a human being.'

Accepting that we go on is *not* just a belief in an afterlife, it's a lifestyle, part of our day-to-day life. The spirit message from a medium is *not* the end of the search for answers, it is the *beginning* of a journey.

Finally, it is a sad but true fact that only a few of us realise our full potential in any one life, and many others believe that so-called 'ordinary' persons must remain ordinary all their lives.

Personally I do not believe *any* human being is ordinary. I believe that everyone has the potential for greatness within them, and everyone of us has the potential to penetrate the thin veil of death and embrace eternity. If, in this lifetime, I succeed in helping just a few people to know that this is true, I will die a happy man, knowing that I have used the gifts I have been given and fulfilled my vocation this time around!

One thing I have learned is that if we seek spiritual values for ourself alone, they turn to dust in our hands; but when we give back what we have received, they multiply and replenish themselves for the greater good of ourselves and all mankind.

With that thought in mind, I am only too happy to have had this opportunity to blend my life with yours. Thank you – and God bless.